WHO KILLED JFK?
THE KENNEDY ASSASSINATION COVER-UP

James R. Duffy

Shapolsky Publishers, Inc.
New York

A Shapolsky Book

First published in the U.S.A. in 1989 by
Shapolsky Publishers
136 West 22nd Street
New York, NY 10011

First published in the U.K. in 1988 by
Alan Sutton Publishing
30 Brunswick Road
Gloucester

Library of Congress Cataloging-in-Publication Data

Duffy, James R.
   Who killed JFK? : the Kennedy assassination cover-up, the web / by
James R. Duffy. — 1st ed.
     p.   cm.
   Bibliography: p.
   ISBN 0-944007-39-2
   1. Kennedy, John F. (John Fitzgerald). 1917–1963 – Assassination.
   2. Oswald, Lee Harvey.   I. Title.
E842.9.D78 1989
973.922'092'4 – dc19   89-6035
                                           CIP

Cover illustration: A still from the Zapruder film of
the Kennedy assassination.
(*Photograph: Colorific*)

INTRODUCTION
by Senator Alfonse M. D'Amato

On the twenty-fifth anniversary of the assassination of President John F. Kennedy, many unanswered questions persist in the collective mind of Americans.

The events of that fateful day have been thoroughly examined, researched and investigated, to the conclusion that Lee Harvey Oswald was the sole triggerman in Dallas. Still, there is a lingering sense that certain facts about Oswald's motivations have eluded us.

Clearly, the national tragedy of the cold-blooded murder of an American President draws us to search for the truth. But our efforts to understand the assassination are magnified by the recognition that the world of 1963 was a very different one from today's.

There was a genuine sense that a grand future of hope and idealism lay ahead of us. With his words, his ideas and, in the age of television, his personal grace, President Kennedy offered his youthful optimism to an eager American public.

In two minutes, one man's actions shattererd those ideals and changed the course of American history.

What drove Lee Harvey Oswald to load his rifle and take aim at the symbol of America's future?

James Duffy's "The Web" studies Oswald's life, associations, and the world in which he immersed himself. It was a contradictory world of Marxist studies, a Marine tour of duty, and defection to the Soviet Union. Oswald allegedly consorted with a wide spectrum of individuals, such as Communists, American patriots, organized crime families, anti-Castro Cuban exiles and the intelligence community.

His bizarre life has been broken down into many parts and studied at length by authors, investigators, and Congressional committees. However, a single, all-encompassing analysis of the numerous and contradictory factors which influenced Lee Harvey Oswald has not yet been adequately addressed.

In a thought-provoking reevaluation of Oswald, Duffy uses his experience as a respected trial lawyer to piece together the reams of information in U.S. Government investigations and reports as the sole basis for his penetrating analysis of the man whose bullets changed America.

"The Web" begins with the emotional instability of Oswald's childhood, and continues through his years of military service, where his strange behavior patterns became more pronounced. As a Marine at a key Air Force base, Oswald flaunted his love for things Russian, exhorting Marxist philosophy and learning and speaking the Russian language. Later, upon his defection to the Soviet Union, Oswald openly alerted U.S. Embassy personnel in Moscow of his intention to disclose sensitive intelligence to the KGB.

Duffy delves into those circumstances and events in Oswald's life which have never been fully explained. We are forced to think about the relative ease with which Oswald entered the Soviet Union, was employed at a Soviet radio factory of great militray interest to the United States, and yet, according to a Soviet defector, was never interrogated by the KGB. Duffy describes Oswald's connections with the henchmen of Fidel Castro, who had his own personal reasons for wanting President Kennedy dead, as well as with organized crime families and anti-Castro Cuban exiles in the U.S.

After his own thorough study of the key individuals and events surrounding Oswald, Duffy readily acknowledges the inability to reach a definitive conclusion. After all, the key answers to the comprehensive truth are buried forever with Oswald.

All that James Duffy asks is that the facts, the contradictions, and the widespread network of Lee Harvey Oswald's associations, which encompass this critical event in our nation's history, be further examined.

A quarter of a century after his assassination, we owe the memory of President John F. Kennedy no less.

Alfonse M. D'Amato
United States Senator
1989

CONTENTS

Excerpts from The Report of the Select
Committee on Assassinations   v

Excerpt from The Report of the President's
Commission on the Assassination of President
Kennedy   vii

Preface   ix

A Word as to Format   xi

Book 1: The Formative Years   1

Book 2: Defector ?   27

Book 3: The Intelligence Connection   97

Book 4: The Web Tightens   177

Sources   238

Notes   240

EXCERPTS FROM

The Report of the Select Committee on Assassinations

US HOUSE OF REPRESENTATIVES

'The Committee believes, on the basis of the evidence available to it, that President John F. Kennedy was probably assassinated as a result of a conspiracy . . .

'Supreme Court Justice Oliver Wendell Holmes once simply defined conspiracy as "a partnership in criminal purposes". That definition is adequate. Nevertheless, it may be helpful to set out a more precise definition. If two or more individuals agreed to take action to kill President Kennedy, and at least one of them took action in furtherance of the plan, and it resulted in President Kennedy's death, the President would have been assassinated as a result of a conspiracy . . .

'Even without physical evidence of conspiracy at the scene of the assassination, there would, of course, be a conspiracy if others assisted Oswald in his efforts. Accordingly, an examination of Oswald's associates is necessary . . .

'It is important to realize, too, that the term "associate" may connote widely varying meanings to different people. A person's associate may be his next door neighbor and vacation companion, or it may be an individual he has met only once for the purpose of discussing a contract for a murder.'

'I think the CIA deliberately deceived the Warren Commission, based on the evidence that I have seen. I think the answer that they have given that they didn't provide the information because nobody asked them is the kind of statement I get from criminal defendants time in and time out . . .'
(House Committee testimony by Judge Burt W. Griffin, formerly Assistant Counsel for the Warren Commission)

EXCERPT FROM

The Report of the President's Commission on the Assassination of President Kennedy (THE WARREN COMMISSION)

'[T]o determine the motives for the assassination of President Kennedy, one must look to the assassin himself.

'Clues to Oswald's motives can be found in his family history, his education or lack of it, his acts, his writings, and the recollections of those who had close contacts with him throughout his life . . .

'[O]thers may study Lee Harvey Oswald's life and arrive at their own conclusions as to his possible motives.'

PREFACE

There have been many – perhaps too many – books purporting to solve the myriad of technical questions which have been raised regarding the tragic events in Dealey Plaza on 22 November 1963 (the number of shots, the angle of fire, the grassy knoll, the Zapruder film, the various wounds, the 'magic bullet', etc.), most of them having as their objective either proving or disproving that Lee Harvey Oswald was the assassin.

This is *not* such a book.

There have been a number of books wherein the writers purport – on the basis of their own personal research and interviews – to reveal some new information about the assassination. Interesting, but in the end totally dependent upon accepting the credibility and impartiality of the authors, who may in fact be merely setting forth their own pet theories.

This is not *that* type of book, either.

What, then, is this book? Or, perhaps more to the point: Why yet another assassination book?

As the introductory quotes suggest, this is a book about Lee Harvey Oswald, his background and his 'associates' – a word not ordinarily employed when discussing this man.

Oswald has, from the time of the assassination, been widely perceived as a somewhat one-dimensional, almost sub-human figure: non-conforming, anti-social, a malcontent, anti-American, an avowed Marxist and Communist, isolated, profoundly alienated, frustrated, resentful, hostile, presumably possessed of less than ordinary intelligence and – perhaps most important of all – he has consistently been portrayed as a 'loner'. To be sure, there is evidence to suggest that he was all of these things.

Yet, scattered through various official US Government documents, there are bits and pieces of information which, when brought together, constitute a substantial body of evidence which permits some rather strikingly different conclusions to be drawn about this notorious but 'unknown' man.

This book, derived wholly and solely from United States Government investigations and reports, narrates all the relevant evidence about Lee Harvey Oswald, points out and discusses the areas of conflict, and leaves the conclusions to the reader.

It tells the arresting story of one of history's most bewildering characters, and the threads seemingly linking him to remarkably diverse groups of people: threads of a web which included intelligence agents and underworld bosses, communists and anti-communists, patriots and spies, big shots and bimbos – a web of bizarre, indeed shocking, activities ranging from infiltration and subversion to assassination plots against the leaders of a number of countries.

It proves once again the old adage that 'Truth is stranger than fiction'.

A WORD AS TO FORMAT

The underlying premise of this book is that within official government reports there is abundant credible evidence to seriously question the accepted wisdom regarding Lee Harvey Oswald. To underscore this assertion, whenever it is consistent with maintaining a readable flow, the text of this work consists of direct quotes from these reports.

A compromise has been attempted as to attribution. On the one hand, this is not a history book and numerous footnotes can prove burdensome and distracting to the person reading for enjoyment. On the other hand, the reader can be confident as to the authenticity of the material only if the sources are specified and can be checked.

Therefore, at the end of the book is a chapter-by-chapter breakdown wherein the source(s) for each topic in that chapter is specifically cited.

Meanwhile, the reader is advised that each and every fact set forth in this book – whether in quotes or not – is drawn directly and exclusively from the following sources:

Report of the President's Commission on the Assassination of President John F. Kennedy, published by the US Government Printing Office in 1964 (known as the Warren Report).

Alleged Assassination Plots Involving Foreign Leaders, conducted by the Select Committee to Study Governmental Operations with respect to Intelligence Activities, United States Senate, published by the US Government Printing Office in 1975.

The Investigation of the Assassination of President John F. Kennedy, conducted by the Senate Select Committee to study Governmental Operations, published by the US Government Printing Office in 1976.

Investigation of the Assassination of President John F. Kennedy, conducted by the Select Committee on Assassinations of the US House of Representatives, published by the US Government Printing Office in 1979.

BOOK 1

THE FORMATIVE YEARS

The Family

Exchange Alley, on the outskirts of the French Quarter, was a rough area. It was the hub of some of the most notorious, openly conducted underworld joints in New Orleans. This narrow bleak street was the location of various gambling operations affiliated to the organization of Carlos Marcello, the city's crime boss. Sordid bars also operated there, including some in which aggressive homosexuals and prostitutes were frequenters.

At 126 Exchange Alley, over the pool hall which was a hangout for gamblers, was a dingy little apartment where, during 1955 and 1956, a teenager named Lee Harvey Oswald lived with his once-widowed, twice-divorced mother.

Marguerite Claverie, born in New Orleans in 1907, had first married one Edward John Pic, jun. in August 1929. By the summer of 1931, she and Pic were separated, though she was then three months pregnant with a son who would be named John Edward Pic.

On 20 July 1933, having obtained a divorce from Pic, Marguerite married Robert Edward Lee Oswald, an insurance premium collector whom she had been seeing during her separation. Mr Oswald's offer to adopt his wife's young son was objected to by Marguerite since that might cut off her support payments from Edward Pic.

A son born to the Oswalds on 7 April 1934 was named Robert Oswald, jun. On 18 October 1939, two months after her husband died suddenly of a heart attack, Marguerite gave birth to the second son of this marriage, naming him Lee after his father and Harvey which was his paternal grandmother's maiden name.

The two older boys, John Pic and Robert Oswald, were soon sent to a Catholic boarding school in Algiers, Louisiana, where they remained for about a year. They then returned home for a while, but on 3 January 1942 their mother placed them in an orphan asylum, known as Bethlehem Children's Home. Marguerite had actually inquired about placing all three boys in the orphanage, but Lee was not accepted because at two years of age he was too young to be admitted.

Marguerite returned to work, leaving Lee for much of the next year with her sister, Mrs Lillian Murret, and at other times with a sitter.

Then, on the day after Christmas, 1942, three-year-old Lee Harvey Oswald was sent to the orphanage.

During the year 1943, Marguerite was dating Edwin A. Ekdahl, and by January 1944 they had decided to marry. Marguerite withdrew Lee from the orphanage and moved with him to Dallas, where Ekdahl expected to be working. John and Robert were thereafter withdrawn from the home and went to live with their mother in Dallas. Marguerite then decided she did not want to marry Ekdahl, though she continued to see him. Finally, however, she and Ekdahl were married in May 1945.

Several months before this, in February 1945, Marguerite had stated that she expected to travel a great deal, and tried to return the older boys to the home. Though she failed in that endeavor, in the fall of that year she succeeded in sending John and Robert away to a military academy where they would live until the summer of 1948.

Concurrent with sending the older boys off to the military academy, the Ekdahls moved to Benbrook, a suburb of Fort Worth, Texas. Lee was immediately entered into the first grade at the Benbrook Common School (whose records show his birth date as 9 July 1939, an incorrect date presumably given by his mother to satisfy the age requirement).

Lee became quite attached to Ekdahl, finding in him the father he never had. But this father-son relationship was to be short-lived, for the marriage between his mother and Ekdahl soon became stormy. Marguerite separated from Ekdahl, and moved with Lee to Covington, Louisiana.

Since Lee had not completed the first grade at Benbrook, in September 1946 he was again entered into the first grade, this time at the Covington Elementary School. He was withdrawn from the Covington School on 23 January 1947 because the Ekdahls, having reconciled, were now moving to Fort Worth. He finally completed first grade in the Clayton Public School and entered second grade at that school the following September. However, relations between the Ekdahls having deteriorated again, Marguerite moved to another location in Fort Worth and Lee completed second grade at the Clark Elementary School.

The Ekdahls were finally divorced in June, 1948, after a bitter trial in which the jury found that Marguerite was guilty of 'excesses, cruel treatment, or outrages' unprovoked by Ekdahl's conduct. The divorce restored to Marguerite her former name, Marguerite C. Oswald.

Mrs Oswald then purchased a small, one-bedroom house in Benbrook and moved in with her three sons. John and Robert slept on the porch, and Lee slept with his mother (a practice which continued until he was almost eleven years old). By the end of the summer, she had sold this house and moved once again into Fort Worth. Lee attended third grade at the Arlington Heights Elementary School, but the following year he was transferred to his sixth school, Ridglea West Elementary School, which he attended for the next three years.

After the divorce, Marguerite complained considerably about how unfairly she was treated, dwelling on the fact that she was a widow with three children. She overstated her financial problems, was unduly concerned about money, and Lee was brought up in an atmosphere of constant money problems.

Marguerite worked in miscellaneous jobs after her divorce from Ekdahl. When she worked during the school year, Lee not only left an empty house in the morning, but returned to it at lunch and then again at night, his mother having trained him to do that rather than to play with other children. Lee seemed to enjoy being by himself and to resent discipline.

In 1950, John entered the Coast Guard, and in July 1952 Robert joined the Marines.

In August 1952, Marguerite and Lee moved to New York City. They lived for a time with John (who was stationed there) and his wife and baby. Marguerite did not get along with John's wife, with whom she quarrelled frequently. In late September, Marguerite and Lee moved to their own apartment.

Lee's truancy soon became a severe problem, and after several unsuccessful attempts were made to resolve the situation, on 12 March 1953 the attendance officer filed a petition in court which ultimately resulted in Lee being remanded to Youth House from 16 April to 7 May for psychiatric study.

The Chief Psychiatrist at Youth House, Dr Renatus Hartogs, summarized his report on Lee by stating: 'This 13-year-old well-built boy has superior mental resources and functions only slightly below his capacity level in spite of chronic truancy from school which brought him into Youth House. No findings of neurological impairment or psychotic mental changes could be made. Lee has to be diagnosed as "personality pattern disturbance with schizoid features and passive-aggressive tendencies". Lee has to be seen as an emotionally, quite disturbed youngster who suffers under the impact of really existing emotional isolation and deprivation, lack of affection, absences of family life and rejection by a self-involved and conflicted mother.'

Mrs Evelyn Strickman Siegel, a social worker who interviewed both Lee and his mother while Lee was confined in Youth House, described him as a 'seriously detached, withdrawn youngster'. She also noted that there was 'a rather pleasant, appealing quality about this emotionally starved, affectionless youngster which grows as one speaks to him'. She thought he had detached himself from the world around him because 'no one in it ever met any of his needs for love'.

Irving Sokolow, a Youth House psychologist, reported that: 'The Human Figure Drawings are empty, poor characterizations of persons approximately the same age as the subject. They reflect a considerable amount of impoverishment in the social and emotional areas. He appears to be a somewhat insecure youngster exhibiting much inclination for warm and satisfying relationships to others. There is some indication that he may relate to men more easily than to women in view of the more mature conceptualization. He appears slightly withdrawn and in view of the lack of detail within the drawings that may assume a more significant characteristic. He exhibits some difficulty in relationship to the maternal figure suggesting more anxiety in this area than in any other.'

Lee scored an IQ of 118 on the Wechsler Intelligence Scale for Children. According to Sokolow, this indicated a 'present intellectual functioning in the upper range of bright normal intelligence'. Sokolow said that although Lee was 'presumably disinterested in school subjects he operates on a much higher than average level'. On the Monroe Silent Reading Test, Lee's score indicated no retardation in reading speed or comprehension; he had better than average ability in arithmetical reasoning for his age group.

On the basis of all the test results, Dr Hartogs recommended that Lee be placed on probation with a requirement that he be provided help and guidance during the probation. However, such help and guidance was never provided, the basic problem being that the few facilities which provided the necessary services already had full case-loads.

On 24 September, the day the probation had originally been scheduled to end, Mrs Oswald phoned the probation officer and said that she could not appear in court, adding that there was no need to do so, as Lee was attending school regularly and was now well adjusted. The probation was extended until 29 October, before which date the school was to submit a progress report. Mrs Oswald's assurances to the contrary notwithstanding, the report, when it was submitted, was a highly unfavorable one.

On 29 October, Mrs Oswald again telephoned to say she would be unable to appear. The probation was continued until 19 November, on which date Lee and his mother appeared. But, despite Mrs Oswald's request that Lee be discharged, Justice Sicher stated his belief that Lee needed treatment, and he continued his probation until 29 January 1954. The probation officer was directed to contact the Big Brothers counseling service in the meantime. On 4 January a caseworker from Big Brothers visited the Oswald home, where he was cordially received, but was told by Mrs Oswald that further counseling was unnecessary.

Mrs Oswald informed the Big Brother caseworker that she intended to return to New Orleans. The caseworker advised her that she must obtain Lee's release from the court's jurisdiction before she left. The next day she called the probation officer. In his absence (he was away on vacation) his office advised Mrs

Oswald not to take Lee out of the jurisdiction without the court's consent. The same advice was repeated to her by the Big Brother caseworker on 6 January. Without further communication to the court (and without him ever getting any of the help or treatment deemed necessary for him) Mrs Oswald took Lee to New Orleans sometime before 10 January.

BOOK 1

CHAPTER

2

Another Kind of 'Family'

Back in New Orleans, Lee and his mother stayed with her sister and brother-in-law, Mr and Mrs Charles Murret, until they got an apartment of their own. Lee had developed a close relationship with the Murrets during his numerous stays with them over the years. Now that he was back in New Orleans, he visited with them regularly, eating dinner with them on Friday evenings and spending his Saturdays there. His uncle Charles Murret was a father figure of sorts. The Murrets served as the closest thing to a real family he had been exposed to up to that point. This special relationship would continue throughout Oswald's life.

Years earlier, Charles Murret (commonly called 'Dutz'), who had been involved in promoting several prize-fighters in New Orleans, had served as the manager of a boxer named Tony Sciambra. After his boxing days, Sciambra had gone on to become a lieutenant to a local organized crime leader named Sam Saia.

'Dutz' Murret later became involved with Saia in an underworld gambling syndicate affiliated to the Carlos Marcello crime family. Saia, who had made his money by dope peddling in the early years, was one of the largest bookmakers in New Orleans, and the financial backer of numerous underworld clubs throughout the New Orleans area. Saia was known to be 'very close' to Carlos Marcello, and it was through the gambling wire service controlled by Marcello that Saia and his associates such as 'Dutz' Murret conducted their betting operations.

Prior to her first marriage, Lee's mother had been working as a secretary for a New Orleans lawyer named Raoul Sere. They became friendly enough that when that marriage failed, Sere re-hired her and helped her pay some debts she had acquired for furniture and other items. This friendship continued into 1960 at the earliest, when Sere took her out to dinner on at least one occasion. In the interim Sere, who was politically active as an attorney, had for a period of time become an assistant district attorney for the city of New Orleans.

Aaron Kohn, chairman of the Metropolitan Crime Commission of New Orleans, has testified that 'Sere played a key role in running the DA's office during the period in which that office was later proven to be highly corrupt' and, 'The DA's office was then under the corrupt influence of the gambling syndicate – Carlos Marcello and various others – to a very significant degree'.

Marguerite had been friends from childhood with another New Orleans attorney, Clem Sehrt, whose law partner counted Carlos Marcello among his clients. Sehrt, a former state banking official, had risen to prominence in Louisiana through his close relationship with Louis J. Rousell, a New Orleans banking executive who was an old and close associate of Carlos Marcello. During the 1950s, when Sehrt's relationship to him was the closest, Rousell had become involved in a political scandal concerning reported cash pay-offs to two Louisiana Supreme Court justices from an unreported corporate payroll of Rousell plus the provision of a new Cadillac each year to the Chief Judge of the Louisiana Supreme Court.

Another of Marguerite's friends (as well as of 'Dutz' Murret and Sam Saia) was Sam Termine, who, according to the New Orleans Metropolitan Crime Commission, was a Louisiana crime figure involved in a number of illicit operations including syndicate gambling and prostitution, as well as in the operation of a motel used for underworld activities. Termine was particularly close to Carlos Marcello, whom he had once served as a chauffeur and bodyguard.

Of the ubiquitous Carlos Marcello, more later.

BOOK 1

CHAPTER

3

Svengali

Upon returning to New Orleans, Lee had been enrolled in the eighth grade at Beauregard Junior High School on 13 January 1954, and he continued there in the ninth grade that September. In September 1955 he entered the tenth grade at Warren Eastern High School.

Meanwhile, in the early summer of 1955, Lee Harvey Oswald had begun attending meetings of the Civil Air Patrol, a student aviation organization which met twice a week. The first unit he was involved with was located at the Lakefront Airport. The commander of that group, who also participated in the training of recruits, was a man named David Ferrie. There was another CAP unit over at Moisant Airport, and by late summer both Lee Oswald and David Ferrie had become attached to that unit. For at least the next few months Lee Harvey Oswald had continued involvement at the Moisant Airport unit of the CAP with David Ferrie.

Born in Cleveland, Ohio in 1918, David Ferrie was 'a complex, even bizarre individual . . . His unusual personal appearance was partially a result of the loss of his body hair induced by a rare disease. He wore a makeshift toupee and exaggerated fake eyebrows affixed crudely with glue as compensation [for his missing hair] . . . Persons who knew him considered him sloppy and unkempt, with a proclivity for foul language . . .

'Although his formal education was not extensive, Ferrie was considered highly intelligent, even brilliant. He had originally studied theology in the hope of becoming an ordained priest, but he left seminary school before graduation because of "emotional instability". Later, in 1941, he received a bachelor of arts degree from Baldwin-Wallace College, majoring in philosophy. He also received, through a correspondence course, a doctorate degree in psychology from an uncredited school, Phoenix University, Bari, Italy . . .

'Ferrie spent considerable time studying medicine and psychology, especially the techniques of hypnosis which he frequently practiced on his young associates.

'Ferrie's major avocation and occupation was flying. Even associates who were critical of Ferrie's character considered him an excellent pilot . . . He took flying lessons at Sky Tech Airway Service in Cleveland, Ohio, between 1942 and 1945, following his failure at the seminary. He then worked as a pilot for an oil drilling firm which had jobs in South America. When the company went out of business, Ferrie tried teaching at Rocky River High School, but was fired in 1948 for psychoanalyzing his students instead of teaching them. Although his exact movements [thereafter] are not known, it appears he had gone to Tampa, Florida, where he received his instrument rating at Sunnyside Flying School. In 1950, Ferrie returned to Cleveland [where] he worked as an insurance inspector . . . In 1951, he submitted an application to Eastern Airlines, omitting details of his past emotional and occupational difficulties. Eastern Airlines hired him in Miami, and soon transferred him to New Orleans.'

David Ferrie was a homosexual and misogynist whose sexual exploitation of younger men was at about this time becoming more and more flagrant. 'He often gave parties at his residence where liquor flowed freely.' On at least one occasion some CAP cadets became drunk at his home and engaged in various activities in the nude. Such incidents led to Ferrie being expelled from the CAP in late 1955.

Over the next few years, a number of different complaints involving his activities with a variety of boys of about fifteen years of age resulted in charges such as 'crimes against nature', 'indecent behavior', and 'contributing to the delinquency of a juvenile'. These ultimately led to his discharge from Eastern Airlines for moral turpitude.

'Many of Ferrie's cadets became involved in Ferrie's wide spectrum of other activities.'

'Ferrie's tremendous influence and close association with these young men eventually became a controversial subject with many parents.'

'He was able to exert tremendous influence over his close associates, including many young men in his Civil Air Patrol squadron.'

'He was rabidly anti-Communist . . . frequently critical of each Presidential administration for what he perceived to be sell-outs to communism.'

'He urged several boys to join the armed forces.'

In October 1955, Lee Harvey Oswald, who had just turned sixteen, dropped out of school and tried to enlist in the Marines, using a false affidavit from his mother stating that he was seventeen. Lee was by all accounts particularly susceptible to the thought of entering the service. His older brothers had both done so, perhaps as a way of escaping from their mother, and Lee himself had seen the service as a way to be on his own, according to Evelyn Strickman, the social worker who had seen him in New York.

The attempted enlistment failed, and according to his mother, Lee spent the next year reading and memorizing the Marine Manual which he had obtained from Robert, and 'living to when he is age 17 to join the Marines'.

Anticipating that Lee would join the Marines as soon as he was seventeen, Mrs Oswald moved in July 1956 to Fort Worth, where Lee was enrolled in the tenth grade at the Arlington Heights High School. Lee became seventeen on 18 October and enlisted in the Marines on 24 October 1956.

At some later date, according to one of Ferrie's colleagues, Jack S. Martin, David Ferrie told him 'about a young friend who had witnessed an alleged "crime against nature" that Ferrie had committed, a young man who had left New Orleans and "subsequently joined the US Marine Corps"'.

The eccentric David Ferrie will reappear later in our story.

BOOK 1

CHAPTER

4

The Chameleon

The period of time, beginning in mid-1955, when he first came into contact with David Ferrie, until October, 1956 when he entered the Marines, marks the emergence of the first in a long series of what appear to be striking inconsistencies in the conduct of Lee Harvey Oswald. Careful evaluation of these seemingly incongruous actions is essential if we can ever hope to discern who or what this chameleonic figure really was like.

At some point during this period, Lee had begun – and had openly flaunted – the reading of Communist literature, surely a curious choice of reading material for one so intent on joining the United States Marine Corps.

The Warren Commission speculated that 'his study of Communist literature, which might appear to be inconsistent with his desire to join the Marines, could have been another manifestation of Oswald's rejection of his environment'. Perhaps so.

But that theory did not take into account that this was an even more curious, more inconsistent activity for someone involved with such a fanatical anti-Communist as David Ferrie. It is indisputable that it did not take this into account because the Warren Commission was not even aware of the Ferrie connection, which came to light many years later.

Therefore, without in any way dismissing the Warren Commission's explanation, which may be completely correct, any rational analysis of this incongruity should, at the very least, consider the relationship between the emotionally-starved, fatherless, young Lee Harvey Oswald, and the Svengali-like David Ferrie.

Though perhaps somewhat more extreme than others, Ferrie's anti-Communism was not unique for the time. Since the end of World War II, the fear of Godless Communism had been a major concern of many Americans. It was the era of the House Unamerican Activities Committee, Senator Joseph McCarthy, the Smith Act, the Internal Security Act of 1950, and the Communist Control Act of 1954.

It was also the era of covert action programs run by the FBI. While the FBI by no means had a monopoly on such anti-Communist covert action programs, they did initiate a new one in 1956, an operation called COINTELPRO, which was their acronym for 'counter-intelligence program'.

Counter-intelligence, an art-form practiced as well by the CIA as the various military intelligence groups, can be defined as those actions by an intelligence agency intended to protect its own security including affirmative action taken to undermine or neutralize hostile intelligence operations.

One contemporaneous example of counter-intelligence (and of the public obsession with Communism) was the highly-popular television series, *I Led Three Lives*, a program which purported to relate the clandestine adventures and triumphs of Herb Philbrick, an FBI undercover agent who had been surreptitiously infiltrated into the Communist Party. According to Lee's mother, *I Led Three Lives* was a steady part of his TV viewing diet.

****

Reading and flaunting Communist literature, while at the same time avidly studying, and wishing his life away until he could join the Marines, was not his only contradictory trait during this time.

On 3 October 1956, just two weeks before the birthday on which he had long planned to leave the Fort Worth area in order to enter the Marines Corps, Lee wrote the following letter to the Socialist Party of America:

Dear Sirs:

I am sixteen years of age and would like more information about your Youth League, I would like to know if there is a branch in my area, how to join, etc. I am a Marxist, and have been studying socialist principles for well over fifteen months. I am very interested in your YPSL.

Sincerely
Lee Oswald

BOOK 1

CHAPTER

5

The Unique Marine

On 26 October 1956, Lee Harvey Oswald reported for duty at the Marine Corps Recruit Depot in San Diego, California. His preference of duty was recorded as Aircraft Maintenance and Repair, the duty assignment for which he was recommended.

Following basic training at San Diego and then at Camp Pendelton, California, Oswald was assigned for additional training, first to the Naval Air Technical Training Center at the Naval Air Station in Jacksonville, Florida, then to Kessler Air Force Base in Biloxi, Mississippi, and then to the Marine Corps Air Station at El Toro, California.

While at San Diego, Oswald was trained in the use of the M-1 rifle. His practice scores were not very good, but somehow when his company fired for record on 21 December, he scored 212, two points above the score necessary to qualify as a 'sharpshooter' on a marksman/sharpshooter/expert scale. (He did not do nearly as well when he fired for record again shortly before he left the Marines.)

It may just have been another case of the service

assigning an Eskimo to the tropics, but it has been perhaps too facilely passed over that the additional training Oswald received at these military locations was as a radar operator; and it was in that capacity that he ultimately came to be assigned to the Marine Air Control Squadron at Atsugi Air Base, 20 miles west of Tokyo, Japan.

Radar, by definition, is 'a method of detecting distant objects and determining their position, velocity, or other characteristics by analysis of very high frequency radio waves reflected from their surfaces'. The training, in addition to radar theory and use, included aircraft surveillance, map reading and air traffic control procedures.

On his aptitude tests, taken on 30 October – which are presumably what would have prompted someone to assign him to this specialty – although Oswald had scored significantly above the Marine Corps averages in reading and vocabularly, significantly *below* the average in arithmetic and pattern analysis, and near the bottom of the lowest group in the radio code test, his composite general classification score was 105, two points below the Corps average. Indeed, he finished the six-week course at Jacksonville forty-sixth in a class of fifty-four students.

Then a most surprising thing happened. At Kessler, following a six-week course during which none of his fellow Marines knew where he spent his free time, except that it was thought to be away from the base, Lee was placed seventh in a class of thirty.

We shall in a subsequent chapter consider whether there could have been some purpose in taking Oswald, despite his aptitude test scores, and qualifying him to be a radar operator.

The specialty of radar operator, even from the training stage, required dealing with confidential material. On 3 May 1957, this young man who had been flaunting an apparent interest in Communist literature was granted a 'confidential' clearance.

Oswald retained his clearance throughout his

enlistment despite the fact that he became more and more blatant in overtly showcasing his interest in Russia – a fact which is rather curious considering that Atsugi Air Base was home to the super-secret U-2 spy plane which took off and landed there.

Most of those who knew him in the Marines, at Atsugi and at the other bases, were able to recount anecdotes which suggested to the Warren Commission that Oswald was anxious to publicize his liking for things Russian, sometimes in good humor and sometimes seriously. Some of his colleagues called him 'Oswaldskovich', apparently to his pleasure. He was said to have had his name written in Russian on one of his jackets; to have played records of Russian songs 'so loud that one could hear them outside the barracks'; frequently to have made remarks in Russian or used expressions like 'da' or 'nyet' or addressed others (and been addressed) as 'Comrade'; to have come over and said jokingly, 'You called?' when one of the marines played a particular record of Russian music. When he played chess, according to one of his opponents he chose the red pieces, expressing a preference for the 'Red Army'. He regularly and openly read a Russian language newspaper; Lieutenant John Donovan thought it was a Communist newspaper and believed Oswald had a subscription to it.

It appeared to most observers that connected with this Russophilia was an interest in and acceptance of Russian political views and Communist ideology. Indeed, Kerry Thornley, a marine who described himself as a close acquaintance but not a good friend of Oswald, thought he definitely believed that 'the Marxist morality was the most rational morality to follow', and Communism 'the best system in the world'.

Oswald the political heretic received even more endorsement as a malcontent with his two court martials in 1957, one for possession of an unauthorized .22 caliber derringer pistol, and the other for verbally assaulting and pouring a drink on a non-commissioned officer. For these offenses his combined punishments cost him $105, a reduction in rank to the grade of private and confinement to hard labor for 48 days.

Most of the marines who knew Lee Oswald were aware that he was studying the Russian language. By 25 February 1959 his studying had progressed to the point that he attempted a foreign language qualification test; his rating of 'poor' on this exam must be evaluated in light of the fact that he was apparently studying on his own. One observer with some knowledge of Russian, Rosaleen Quinn, thought he spoke the language well in view of his lack of formal training.

Oswald's fellow marines at his various units can provide little if any information as to his activities when not actually on the base and in the unit. Throughout his tour of duty, Oswald invariably tended to disappear from the view of his fellow marines during off-hours, weekends and leaves.

In November 1958 Oswald finished his overseas tour of duty, and was shipped back to California; after travel time and thirty-day leave, he was assigned to a Marine Air Control Squadron at the Marine Corps Air Station at El Toro, where he had been based briefly before he went overseas.

In March 1959, Oswald took a series of high-school level general level educational development tests, and received an overall rating of 'satisfactory'. In the same month, he applied to Albert Schweitzer College in Churwalden, Switzerland, for admission to the spring term in 1960. This application was approved by the college, and by letter dated 19 June, Oswald sent his registration fee of $25.

Lee was obligated to serve on active duty until 7 December 1959 (the date having been adjusted to compensate for the period of confinement). But then, in August, he made a voluntary allotment of $40 to his mother, applied for a dependant's quarters ('Q') allotment on her behalf, and on 17 August he submitted a request for a dependency discharge on the ground that his mother needed his support due to an injury she had sustained at work (there had been an injury the previous December). Within two weeks, the application had been approved.

This is one of a number of occasions when Lee Harvey Oswald appeared to be remarkably expeditious in cutting through red tape, ostensibly because this unintelligent non-conformist somehow seemed to always have his papers complete and in order.

But it so happens that this particular application was not truly complete. Although the requisite preconditions of a voluntary allotment and request for 'Q' allotment had been made, and although the application was accompanied by an affidavit of Mrs Oswald and corroborating affidavits from an attorney, a doctor, and two friends, all the supporting affidavits for the quarters allotment had not been submitted at the time the hardship discharge application was filed. Nonetheless, the application was quickly forwarded, with merely an endorsement that the reviewing officers were aware that both the requisite voluntary contribution and the application for a quarters allotment had been made.

However, under the applicable procedures, Oswald's requisite application for a quarters allowance for his mother should have been disallowed because he had not contributed any money to her during the preceding year. Moreover, the reviewing officer in his endorsement, dated 19 August (only two days after it was submitted), stated 'A genuine hardship exists in this case, and in my opinion approval of the "Q" allotment will not sufficiently alleviate this situation.'

This is a puzzling statement in light of the fact that the Fort Worth Red Cross office indicated that only a quarters allotment was necessary for Marguerite Oswald, rather than a hardship discharge for Lee. On 28 August, the Wing Hardship or Dependency Discharge Board recommended that Oswald's request for a discharge be approved, which was done shortly thereafter.

On 4 September, pending his hardship discharge so he could go home and support his injured mother, Lee Oswald applied for a passport. His application stated that he planned to leave the United States on 21 September to attend the Albert Schweitzer College and the University of Turku in Finland, as well as to travel in Cuba, the Dominican Republic, England, France, Germany, and Russia. The passport was issued six days later.

Oswald received his hardship discharge on 11 September. He arrived in Fort Worth by 14 September, gave his mother $100, and departed three days later for New Orleans.

BOOK 2

DEFECTOR ?

BOOK 2

CHAPTER

6

Destination Golub

The Warren Commission, utilizing Oswald's own 'Historic Diary' together with various documents and testimony from Russian and American sources, reconstructed a rather detailed account of his defection to, and life in, the Soviet Union.

In summary, according to this account, Lee Harvey Oswald sought to defect to Russia; was rejected; became despondent, and attempted suicide, which resulted in the Russians accepting him; was sent to an obscure job in an obscure city; grew dissatisfied with Russian life; and thereupon re-defected to the United States, having in the meantime acquired a Russian wife.

Information has subsequently emerged which demonstrates that there are significant problems with each of the sources for this account, and which therefore suggests that the above scenario may be totally untrue.

Indeed, one of the questions which arise is: Could it be that Lee Harvey Oswald was actually an agent of the United States, and that his defection to Russia was for some mission of the US?

What follows below is the Warren Commission reconstruction supplemented by the more recent evidence and observations.

According to the Warren Report: 'On 17 September, Oswald spoke with a representative of Travel Consultants, Inc., a New Orleans travel bureau; he filled out a "Passenger Immigration Questionnaire" on which he gave his occupation as "shipping export agent", and said that he would be abroad for 2 months on a pleasure trip. He booked passage from New Orleans to Le Havre, France, on a freighter, the SS *Marion Lykes*, scheduled to sail on 18 September, for which he paid $220.75. On the evening of 17 September, he registered at the Liberty Hotel.

'The *Marion Lykes* did not sail until the early morning of 20 September . . . [It] carried only four passengers. Oswald shared his cabin with Billy Joe Lord, a young man who had just graduated from high school and was going to France to continue his education . . . The other two passengers were Lieutenant Colonel and Mrs George B. Church . . ..

'Oswald disembarked at Le Havre on 8 October. He left for England that same day, and arrived on 9 October. He told English customs officials in Southampton that he had $700 and planned to remain in the United Kingdom for 1 week before proceeding to a school in Switzerland. But on the same day he flew to Helsinki, Finland, where he registered at the Torni Hotel; on the following day, he moved to the Klaus Kurki Hotel. Oswald probably applied for a visa at the Russian Consulate on 12 October, his first business day in Helsinki. The visa was issued on 14 October . . . He left Helsinki by train on the following day, crossed the Finnish-Russian border at Vainikkala, and arrived in Moscow on 16 October . . . He was met at the Moscow railroad station by a representative of "Intourist", the state tourist agency, and taken to the Hotel Berlin, where he registered as a student '

There are noteworthy difficulties with the above scenario.

The circumstances surrounding Oswald's trip from London to Helsinki are most suspicious and mysterious. Oswald's passport indicates he arrived in Finland on 10 October, 1959, and the Torni Hotel in Helsinki has him registered as a guest on that same date.

However, unless Oswald received some well-placed help, there was no way that he could have been registered at the Torni on the same day he arrived in Finland. That is true because of two immutable facts, which no investigation has found to be in error or in dispute:

(1) the only direct flight from London to Helsinki landed at 11.33 p.m. on that date; and,

(2) as conceded in a memorandum by the then CIA Deputy Director, Richard M. Helms, '[i]f Oswald had taken this flight, he could not normally have cleared customs and landing formalities and reached the Torni Hotel downtown by 24.00 (midnight) on the same day'.

Louis Hopkins, the travel agent who arranged for Oswald's passage from the United States, was not aware of Oswald's ultimate destination and so had nothing to do with the London–Helsinki trip. Moreover, Hopkins has testified, had he known Oswald's ultimate destination, his advice would have been to sail not on the *Marion Lykes*, but on a different ship to a port more convenient for Russia.

The mystery is enhanced by Louis Hopkins' observation that Oswald did not appear to be particularly well-informed about travel in Europe.

Further questions arise from Oswald's obtaining a Soviet entry visa within only two days of having applied for it on 12 October, 1959 (10 October, the date of arrival, having been a Saturday, the first opportunity to apply for a visa would have been on Monday, 12 October).

Normally at least a week would elapse between the time of a tourist's application and the issuance of a visa.

This minimum time was, if anything, all the more necessary if, in addition to the processing of the visa application, lodgings were to be arranged through Soviet Intourist, as appears to have been the case with Oswald, inasmuch as he was met at the Moscow railroad station by an Intourist representative and taken to the Hotel Berlin.

However, the Soviet Consul in Helsinki, Gregory Golub, was suspected by American intelligence of also being an officer in the Soviet KGB. Golub had once disclosed in a luncheon conversation that Moscow had given him authority to give Americans visas without prior approval from Moscow, and that 'as long as he was convinced the American was "all right", he could give him a visa in a matter of minutes'.

An American Embassy dispatch, dated 9 October 1959, the day before Oswald arrived in Helsinki, illustrates that Golub indeed had such authority (while at the same time, it prompts some intriguing questions). The dispatch, which had been referring to an earlier telephone contact between Golub and the American Embassy in Helsinki, goes on to state: '. . . Since that evening [4 September 1959] Golub has only phoned [the US consul] once and this was on a business matter. Two Americans were in the Soviet Consulate at the time and were applying for Soviet visas thru Golub. They had previously been in the American consulate inquiring about the possiblilty of obtaining a Soviet visa in 1 or 2 days. [The US Consul] advised them to go directly to Golub and make their request, which they did. Golub phoned [the US Consul] to state that he would give them their visas as soon as they made advance Intourist reservations. When they did this, Golub immediately gave them their visas . . .'

The House Select Committee, which developed this evidence about Golub, concluded: 'Thus, based upon these two factors, (1) Golub's authority to issue visas to

Americans without prior approval from Moscow, and (2) a demonstration of this authority, as reported in an embassy dispatch approximately 1 month prior to Oswald's appearance at the Soviet Embassy, the Committee found that the available evidence tends to support the conclusion that the issuance of Oswald's tourist visa within 2 days after his appearance at the Soviet Consulate was not indicative of an American intelligence agency connection.' And, in a footnote, they observed: 'If anything, Oswald's ability to receive a Soviet entry visa so quickly was more indicative of a Soviet interest in him.'

This footnote is puzzling in the extreme, since it appears to be inconsistent with the very conclusion it footnotes. That conclusion makes crystal-clear that Oswald's ability to receive a Soviet entry visa so quickly had absolutely nothing to do with a Soviet interest in him; that, in fact, its speedy issuance would indicate that it was not cleared in Moscow (a presumption which the reader might find even more compelling when we discuss the less-than-enthusiastic reception Oswald received in Moscow).

However, the conclusion itself is, if anything, more puzzling than the footnote. What the conclusion really amounts to is a statement that there is no American intelligence agency connection, since we have evidence that the expedited visa was issued by Golub.

But the premise does not support the conclusion. The probable involvement of Golub in the issuance of Oswald's expedited – and uninvestigated – visa does not eliminate the possibility of American intelligence agency involvement; it may, in fact, make such involvement more likely.

Logically, it should be the beginning of a line of inquiry that asks the simple question: Why Golub?

The above cited evidence would seem to justify the following speculative queries on that score:

(1) If the United States wished to infiltrate someone into the Soviet Union, would it be helpful if the

necessity of prior clearance from Moscow for his visa could be circumvented?

(2) Did the United States know that the necessity of prior visa clearance from Moscow could be circumvented via Gregory Golub?

(3) If (hypothetically) the United States wished to infiltrate a Lee Harvey Oswald into the Soviet Union, would it make sense to steer him to Gregory Golub?

(4) Might 'Destination Golub' explain Oswald's odyssey from New Orleans to Le Havre to London to Helsinki, instead of proceeding to a port more convenient for Russia?

(5) If the answers to the last four questions appear to be in the affirmative, may it be that the Committee has actually proven the exact opposite of the conclusion it has stated?

In other words, might 'Destination Golub' point to involvement of the US intelligence community in Oswald's defection?

BOOK 2

CHAPTER

7

Russia

The Warren Commission reconstruction indicates that on the day after his arrival in Moscow, Oswald told Rima Shirokova, the young woman assigned by Intourist as his guide during his stay in Russia, that he wanted to leave the United States and become a citizen of the Soviet Union. He then sent a letter to the Supreme Soviet requesting that he be granted citizenship.

On 21 October, an official of the Passport and Visa Department notified Oswald that his visa had expired and that he had to leave Moscow within two hours. Oswald responded to this unfavorable decision by cutting himself above the left wrist in an apparent suicide attempt which resulted in his being taken to the Botkinskaya Hospital where he was confined for three days in the psychiatric ward before being transferred to the 'somatic' ward. He was released from the hospital on 28 October.

Oswald now checked out of the Hotel Berlin and registered at the Metropole. His visa had expired while he was in the hospital, and his presence in Russia was technically illegal; he had received no word that the decision that he must leave had been reversed. Later that day, however, an official at the Pass and Registration Office sent for him, and asked whether he still wanted to become a Soviet citizen. Oswald replied in the affirmative, and provided his Marine Corps discharge papers for identification. He was told that he could not expect a decision soon, and was dismissed. For the next three days, he remained in his room, near the phone, fully dressed and ready to leave immediately if summoned.

Then, on the afternoon of 31 October, he apparently decided to act. He took a taxi to the American Embassy, where he asked to see the consul. When the receptionist asked him first to sign the tourist register, he laid his passport on the desk and said that he had come to 'dissolve his American citizenship'.

Richard E. Snyder, the second secretary and senior consular official, was summoned, and he invited Oswald into his office. There, with Snyder's assistant John A. McVickar also present, Oswald declared that he wanted to renounce his American citizenship; he denounced the United States and praised the Government of the Soviet Union. Over Oswald's objections, Snyder sought to learn something of Oswald's motives and background and to forestall immediate action. Oswald stated his admiration for the system and policies of the Soviet Union and his desire to serve the Soviet State; and at one point alluded to hardships endured by his mother as a 'worker', saying he did not intend to let this happen to him.

Oswald informed Snyder that he had been a radar operator in the Marine Corps, intimating that he might know something of special interest, and that he had informed a Soviet official that he would give the Soviets any information he possessed.

Oswald handed to Snyder a note which suggests that he had studied and sought to comply with section 349 of the Immigration and Nationality Act (which provides for the loss of American citizenship) since the note attempts to cast off citizenship in three of the ways specified by the statute.

The interview ended when Snyder told Oswald that he could renounce his citizenship on the following Monday, two days later, if he would appear personally. Snyder has testified that he was attempting to delay Oswald's decision so as to give him a chance to reconsider before making such a step.

Oswald returned to the hotel angry about the delay, but 'elated' by the 'showdown' and sure that he would be permitted to remain after his 'sign of faith' in the Russians.

His sign of faith in the Russians was not to remain a secret for very long. No sooner had he left these closed offices (it being Saturday), than the Embassy – which supposedly was giving Oswald time for cool reflection – sought out and notified the press of the defection.

Soon after he returned to the hotel, he was approached by A. I. Goldberg, a reporter for the Associated Press, and later that day by two other reporters, R. J. Korengold and Aline Mosby. He answered a few questions for the latter two, but refused to be interviewed at this time (though a few weeks later he did give an interview to Miss Mosby of United Press International in which among other things he referred again to his mother's poverty).

A few days after his Saturday visit, the Embassy received a letter from Oswald dated 3 November which requested that his citizenship be revoked. The Embassy replied on 9 November that he could renounce his citizenship by appearing at the Embassy and executing the necessary papers.

Both on 8 November, in a letter to his brother Robert, and on 13 November, in the interview with Aline Mosby, Oswald stated that he had been told that he could remain in the Soviet Union. This conflicts with his diary which states that he was not told until later that he could even remain temporarily. Indeed, according to his diary it was this 'comforting news' that prompted him to grant a second interview on 16 November, this time with Priscilla Johnson of the North American Newspaper Alliance.

When, during this interview, Miss Johnson suggested that if Oswald really wished to renounce his American citizenship he could do so by returning to the Embassy, he said he would 'never set foot in the Embassy again', since he was sure he would be given the 'same run-around' as before.

Miss Johnson's seemingly curious advice from one American to another was followed by her reporting to the Embassy on the next day that she thought that Oswald 'may have purposely not carried through his original intent to renounce in order to leave a crack open'.

Apparently Miss Johnson was not the only reporter to get strange vibes about this attempted renunciation of American citizenship. The Warren Commission related that 'reporters noticed Oswald's apparent ambivalence in regard to renouncing his citizenship – stormily demanding that he be permitted to renounce while failing to follow through by completing the necessary papers. [. . .] He seemed to be avoiding effective renunciation, consciously or unconsciously, in order to preserve his right to re-enter the United States. [. . .] . . . if he had expatriated himself his eventual return to the United States would have been much more difficult and perhaps impossible'.

On 4 January, Oswald was summoned to the Soviet Passport Office and given Identity Document for Stateless Persons No. 311479. He was told that he was being sent to Minsk, an industrial city located about 450 miles southwest of Moscow, with a population at that time of about 510,000. On the following day, he went to a Government agency which the Russians call the 'Red Cross'; it gave him 5,000 rubles (about $500). He used 2,200 rubles to pay his hotel bill and 150 rubles to purchase a railroad ticket to Minsk, where he arrived on 7 January. On the following day he met the 'Mayor', who welcomed him to Minsk and promised him a rent-free apartment.

Oswald reported for work at the Belorussian Radio and Television Factory on 13 January. The factory, a major producer of electronic parts and systems, employed about 5,000 persons. His salary varied from 700 to perhaps as high as 900 rubles per month ($70 – $90), a salary which was normal for his type of work. It was supplemented, however, by 700 rubles per month which he received from the 'Red Cross', and, according to Oswald, his total income was about equal to that of the director of the factory. In August he applied for membership of the union; he became a dues-paying member in September.

Undoubtedly more noteworthy to most Russians than his extra income was the attractive apartment which Oswald was given in March 1959. It was a small flat with a balcony overlooking the river, for which he paid only 60 rubles a month. Oswald describes it in his diary as 'a Russian dream'. Had Oswald been a Russian worker, he would probably have had to wait for several years for a comparable apartment, and would have been given one then only if he had a family. The 'Red Cross' subsidy and the apartment were typical of the favorable treatment which the Soviet Union has given defectors.

Oswald's diary records that he enjoyed his first months in Minsk. His work at the factory was easy and his co-workers were friendly and curious about life in the United States. He dated frequently, attending the theater, a movie, or an opera almost every night. He wrote in his diary 'I'm living big and am very satisfied'.

The spring and summer passed easily and uneventfully. There were picnics and drives in the country, which Oswald described as 'green beauty'. On 18 June, he obtained a hunting licence and soon afterwards he purchased a 16 gauge single-barrel shotgun. He joined a local chapter of the Belorussian Society of Hunters and Fishermen, a hunting club sponsored by his factory, and hunted for small game in the farm regions around Minsk about half a dozen times in the summer and fall, spending the night in small villages. (Parenthetically, Russian records contain statements from fellow hunters that Oswald was an extremely poor shot and it was necessary for persons who accompanied him on hunts to provide him with game.) According to his diary, at about this period of time he felt 'uneasy inside' after a friend took him aside at a party and advised him to return to the United States. In another entry he writes, 'I have become habituated to a small cafe which is where I dine in the evening. The food is generally poor and always exactly the same menu in any cafe at any point in the city. The food is cheap and I don't really care about quality after three years in the USMC.' (Note: Oswald's numerous spelling errors are omitted throughout this book.)

According to Russian records, on 4 January 1961, one year after he had been issued his 'stateless' residence permit, Oswald was summoned to the passport office in Minsk; was asked if he still wanted to become a Soviet citizen; replied that he did not, but asked that his residence permit be extended for another year.

The entry in his diary for 4–31 January reads, 'I am starting to reconsider my desire about staying. The work is drab. The money I get has nowhere to be spent. No nightclubs or bowling alleys, no places of recreation except the trade-union dances. I have had enough.'

On 25 January, Mrs Marguerite Oswald appeared at the State Department in Washington, DC, where she spoke with a Mr Boster and a Mr Hickey. She has testified that she told these men that she was under the impression that her son, Lee, was a US agent, and that she was destitute and just getting over a sickness.

On 1 February 1961, the Department of State in Washington forwarded to the Moscow Embassy a request informing the Embassy that Oswald's mother was worried about him, and asking that he get in touch with her, if possible (which is not exactly what her pitch was).

Then on 13 February 1961, the American Embassy in Moscow received a letter from Oswald postmarked Minsk on 5 February, asking that he be readmitted to the United States.

Considering the timing of the State Department message and Oswald's letter, the Warren Commission opined that 'the simultaneity of the two events was apparently coincidental'. The basis for this conclusion is stated to be that, 'The request from Marguerite Oswald went from Washington to Moscow by sealed diplomatic pouch and there was no evidence that the seal had been tampered with. The officer of the Department of State who carried the responsibility for such matters has testified that the message was not forwarded to the Russians after it arrived in Moscow.'

Obviously, if a message from Mrs Oswald was removed in Moscow from a sealed diplomatic pouch but never forwarded to the Russians, it could bear no cause and effect relationship to Lee's letter. In theory, Mrs Oswald's message would still be lying around the Embassy someplace when Lee's letter arrived. However, if we move from the text of the Warren Report and go instead to Appendix XV, we find that what went to the Moscow Embassy was not a message from private citizen, Marguerite Oswald, to private citizen, Lee Oswald. Quite the contrary, the message was from the State Department to the Moscow Embassy and it read: 'The Embassy is requested to inform the [Soviet] Ministry of Foreign Affairs that Mr Oswald's mother is worried as to his present safety, and is anxious to hear from him.' In this Appendix, it is asserted that this request had not been acted upon by the 13th because the diplomatic pouch which left Washington for Moscow on the 1st did not reach Moscow until the 10th or 11th.

Within Oswald's letter is a statement which, if true, would preclude any possibility of a link between his letter and the State Department missive. That statement is in the form of a complaint by Oswald in this letter that he had written an earlier letter which had not been answered. However, the Warren Commission found that there is evidence that such a letter was never sent – specifically, Oswald's diary refers to this February letter as his 'first request'.

Oswald's letter noted that he did not appear personally because he could not leave Minsk without permission. The Second Secretary, Richard Snyder, answered on 28 February that Oswald would have to appear at the Embassy personally to discuss his return to the United States. A second letter from Oswald, posted on 5 March, reached the Embassy on 20 March; it reiterated that he was unable to leave Minsk without permission, and asked that preliminary inquiries be put in the form of a questionnaire and sent to him.

The Warren Commission noted that, 'The Soviet authorities had undoubtedly intercepted and read the correspondence between Oswald and the Embassy and knew of his plans. Soon after the correspondence began, his monthly payments from the "Red Cross" were cut off.'

Sometime in the second week of March, Miss Katherine Mallory, who was on tour in Minsk with the University of Michigan Symphonic Band, found herself surrounded by curious Russian citizens. A young man who identified himself as a Texan and former Marine stepped out of the crowd and asked if she needed an interpreter; he interpreted for her for the next 15 or 20 minutes. Later he told her that he despised the United States and hoped to stay in Minsk for the rest of his life. Miss Mallory was unable to swear that her interpreter was Oswald, but was personally convinced that it was he.

A few days later, probably on 17 March, Oswald attended a dance at the Palace of Culture for Professional Workers in Minsk, where he met 19-year-old Marina Nikolayevna Prusakova. They met again at another dance a week later, danced together most of the evening, and when he walked her home they arranged to meet again the following week.

However, on Thursday, 30 March, Oswald was admitted to the Clinical Hospital, where Marina worked as a pharmacist. By the time he left the hospital on 11 April, he had asked her to be his fiancée, and she had agreed to consider it.

After his discharge from the hospital he visited Marina regularly at her aunt and uncle's apartment, where she had lived since the previous fall (she never knew her father; her mother died in 1957, and she subsequently left her stepfather with whom she did not get along).

By 20 April, they had filed notice with the registrar of their intent to marry, and had obtained the special consent necessary for an alien to marry a citizen. After waiting the usual ten days, they were married on 30 April.

Marina testified that when she agreed to marry Oswald, she believed – based upon his statements to her – that he did not intend to, and indeed could not, return to the United States. Oddly enough, this would also have to mean that nothing was said to Marina when she applied for permission to marry this alien who the authorities knew was intending to leave the country.

But of greater curiosity is the fact that this would have to mean that her intended's plans to leave the country were kept from her by the beloved uncle with whom she lived, for that uncle was not some ordinary, uninformed soviet citizen – on the contrary, her uncle, Colonel Ilya Vasilyevich Prusakov, was a high-ranking official in the Minsk MVD.

Oswald's diary says that he told Marina 'in the last days of June' that he was anxious to return to the United States. Yet, on 25 May, the Moscow Embassy received a letter mailed in Minsk about ten days earlier, in which Oswald asked for assurances that he would not be prosecuted if he returned, and informing the

Embassy that he had married a Russian woman who would seek to accompany him to the United States. At about this time, the Oswalds began to make inquiries in Soviet offices about exit visas.

It is interesting to note Oswald's social activities at this time. Among his stated reasons for wanting to leave the Soviet Union were complaints about the sameness of the food, and the complaint that there were no places of recreation. Yet, the Warren Commission relates that, 'While these preparations were being made, the Oswalds apparently enjoyed their new life. They ate most of their meals in cafes or at restaurants where they worked. For amusement they went boating, attended the opera, concerts, the circus, and films; occasionally, they gathered with a group of friends for a cooperative meal at someone's apartment.'

Weeks went by, but Lee received no response to his letter informing the Embassy of his desire to bring his new bride with him to the United States. Then, on 8 July, he appeared at the Embassy in Moscow. It being Saturday, the offices were closed.

He used the house telephone to reach Snyder, who came to the office, talked with him briefly, and suggested that he return on the following Monday. Oswald called Marina and asked her to join him in Moscow, which she did, arriving on Sunday.

At the Embassy on Monday, Marina waited outside during Oswald's interview with Snyder, who asked to see his Soviet papers and questioned him closely about his life in Russia and possible expatriating acts. Oswald stated that he was not a citizen of the Soviet Union and had never formally applied for citizenship, that he had never taken an oath of allegiance to the Soviet Union, and that he was not a member of the factory trade union organization. He said that he had never given Soviet officials any confidential information that he had learned in the Marines, had never been asked to give such information, and 'doubted' that he would have done so had he been asked.

The Warren Commission concluded that 'Some of Oswald's statements during this interview were undoubtedly false. He had almost certainly applied for citizenship in the Soviet Union and, at least for a time, been disappointed when it was denied. He possessed a membership card in the union organization. In addition, his assertion to Snyder that he had never been questioned by Soviet authorities concerning his life in the United States is simply unbelievable.'

Snyder concluded that Oswald had not expatriated himself and returned to him his passport, stamped valid only for direct travel to the United States. Accompanied by his wife, Lee came to the Embassy again on the following day to initiate procedures for her admission to the United States as an immigrant.

Marina has testified that when the news of her visit to the American Embassy reached Minsk, she was dropped from membership in 'Komsomol', the Communist Youth Organization, and that 'meetings were arranged' at which 'members of the various organizations' attempted to dissuade her from leaving the Soviet Union. She also says that her aunt and uncle did not speak to her for 'a long time'. Indeed, Lee wrote to the Embassy on 4 October to request that the US Government officially intervene to facilitate his and his wife's applications for exit visas. He stated that there had been systematic and concerted attempts to intimidate Marina into withdrawing her application for a visa, which had resulted in her being hospitalized for a five-day period on 22 September for nervous exhaustion.

There is no record of such hospitalization and Marina agrees there was no such hospitalization. As to the rest of the harrassment and outrage, if it was sincere and not for show, it makes even more incomprehensible the apparently blasé approach of the authorities and her uncle to her courtship by and marriage to Oswald after he had applied for readmission to the United States.

The Embassy replied to Oswald's letter on 12 October, saying that it had no way of influencing Soviet conduct on such matters and that its experience had been that action on applications for exit visas was 'seldom taken rapidly'.

On 25 December 1961, Marina was called to the local passport office in Minsk, where she was told that authority had been received to issue exit visas to her and her husband. The Oswalds did not pick up their exit visas immediately, one reason probably being the fact that Marina was pregnant with their first child, June, who was born on 15 February.

In the meantime, the American Embassy in a letter dated 5 January suggested that since there might be difficulties in obtaining an American visa for Marina, Oswald should consider returning alone and bringing her over later. He replied on the 16th that he would not leave Russia without her. There was apparently less urgency about the departure for the United States after June was born, as Oswald wrote to his mother and brother that he would probably not arrive for several months.

On 1 June, Oswald signed a promissory note at the Embassy for a repatriation loan of $435.71. He and his family boarded a train for Holland, passing through Minsk that night. They crossed the Soviet frontier at Brest on 2 June. Two days later they departed from Holland on the SS *Maasdam*, which landed at Hoboken, New Jersey, on 13 June, where they were met by Spas T. Raikin, a representative of the Travelers Aid Society, which had been contacted by the Department of State. The society referred the Oswalds to the New York City Department of Welfare, which helped them find a room at the Times Square Hotel. On the afternoon of 14 June, the Oswalds left New York by plane for Fort Worth.

BOOK 2

CHAPTER

8

The Diary That Wasn't

It has been pointed out that there are significant problems with each of the sources utilized to reconstruct Oswald's thoughts and activities while in the Soviet Union.

For many years Oswald's 'Historic Diary' was the virtually unchallenged primary source of information on this period of his life, purporting, as it does, to be his contemporaneous documentation of events.

However, some skeptics pointed to certain entries in the diary which they said reflected information which could only have become known after the supposed time of the entries.

The House Select Committee on Assassinations had a number of documents about which there were various questions; inevitably, Oswald's diary came to be amongst them.

In order to resolve these questions, the Committee first asked the President of the American Society of Questioned Document Examiners for his recommendations on the leading experts in the field of questioned document examination, specifically handwritten documents. The Committee then asked each of the people he recommended for their suggestions as to whom the Committee might retain for these purposes. Three names appeared consistently. After ascertaining that none had had a connection with the FBI or the Kennedy case, the Committee requested that this impartial panel undertake an examination of various documents.

The panel members, all of whom belonged to the American Society of Questioned Document Examiners, were Joseph P. McNally, David J. Purtell and Charles C. Scott. The Committee stated their qualifications thus:

'McNally received a BS and an MPA in police science from the John Jay College of Criminal Justice, University of New York City in 1967 and 1975 respectively. He started in the field of questioned document identification in 1942 with the New York Police laboratory. He has been supervisor of the document identification section of the police laboratory, training officer in the police academy, commanding officer of the police laboratory, and handwriting expert in the district attorney's office of New York County. He retired from the police department with the rank of captain in 1972 and entered private practice. He serves as a consultant to New York's Human Resources Administration. McNally is a fellow of the American Academy of Forensic Sciences, and a member of the International Association for Identification, and the American Society for Testing and Materials. He has lectured at the University of New York City, Rockland College, and the New York Police Academy. [. . .]

'Purtell received a Ph.B, with a major in mathematics and chemistry, from Northwestern University in 1949. He began his career in questioned document identification in 1942 with the Chicago Police Department, where he served as document examiner in the scientific crime detection laboratory. He retired in 1974 as chief document examiner and captain of police, and entered private practice in 1973. He is a fellow of the

American Academy of Forensic Sciences and served as chairman of the questioned document section and chairman of the program committee. He is past vice president and president of the American Society of Questioned Document Examiners. Purtell has lectured at Northwestern University, the University of Illinois, the University of Indiana and St Joseph's College, among other schools. He has presented and published numerous scientific papers. [. . .]

'Scott received an AA degree from Kansas City Junior College in 1930 and a JD from the University of Missouri School of Law in 1935, whereupon he became a member of the Missouri bar. While attending law school, he founded the *University of Missouri at Kansas City Law Review* and was its first editor-in-chief. He began his career as a questioned document examiner with the Federal Reserve Bank in 1935 and has been in private practice since 1946. The first edition of his three-volume book, *Photographic Evidence*, was published in 1942. Now in its second edition, it has become the standard textbook on the subject. He served on the first board of directors of the American Board of Forensic Document Examiners. He has conducted seminars on scientific document examination for more than 20 State bar associations, written numerous professional articles, and, since 1954, has been an adjunct professor of law at the University of Missouri School of Law.'

The panel followed standard procedures and techniques in its examinations. The writings and signatures were looked at individually and in juxtaposition with each other, taking into consideration the gross characteristics of the writing process, writing skill, slant, speed, proportions of the letters, ratio of small to capital letters, height ratio, lateral spacing, and overall writing pattern. Significant differences were looked for. A stereoscope microscope was used for minute examination and comparison of individual letters and characteristics.

One of the issues addressed to these experts queried 'Was the "historic diary" written in one sitting?' As to this, the panel concluded that, 'Because of the poor condition of the historical diary, they are unable to conclude firmly whether it was written at one or more than one sitting. On balance, it appears to have been written at one or a few sittings.'

The problem referred to regarding the condition of the diary can best be understood from the comments of David J. Purtell: 'With respect to the timespan of the historical diary, an answer cannot be provided because of the present condition of the paper. The documents had been processed by the silver nitrate method in an attempt to develop latent fingerprints. While a recognized method, the drawback is that it soils the paper; the silver nitrate which remains on the paper causes it to turn black in time. Today, the pages are in very poor condition, and though the message can be read in part, it is a very difficult task. One observation that can be reported is that one sheet of paper is of a different weight (thickness) than the other sheets.'

However, although scientifically dating the age of the writing might have proven helpful, inability to do so did not prevent addressing the truly crucial issue, which might be stated in the question: 'Was this document an accumulation of random entries each entry having been made on the date indicated contemporaneous with the events being recorded?'

As to that very important question, the answer is most unsettling, for it appears to be rather clear that this document, upon which so much reliance has been placed in reconstructing the defection, is a phony. In other words, Lee Harvey Oswald's 'diary' was not a diary at all.

As Joseph P. McNally reported, 'A check was made of the historical diary. The 12 pages were written with the same type of writing instrument. The paper used for 11 of the 12 pages is similar; only the last page differs – it is appreciably thinner. The writing has a continuity from page to page and line to line that is indicative of being written about, or at, the same time. It does not give the impression of being "random", as would be expected of a diary extended over a period of time. It appears that this diary has been written within a short period of time and not over any extensive period.'

This determination not only calls into question the entire reconstruction of Oswald's life in Russia, but also gives rise to a most disturbing new question: 'Why?'

BOOK 2

CHAPTER

9

Yuri Nosenko, KGB Defector

Some CIA agents, including a Chief of Counter-Intelligence in the Agency's Soviet Branch, told the House Select Committee on Assassinations in 1978 that they believed it was possible that Lee Harvey Oswald had been recruited by the Soviet KGB during his military tour at Atsugi Air Base in Japan, as the CIA had identified a KGB program aimed at recruiting US military personnel during the period Oswald was stationed there.

This was not a new concern. From the time of his arrest for the killing of President Kennedy, a primary concern was the question: 'Had Oswald been enlisted by the Soviet secret police, the dreaded KGB?'

Then, in February 1964, only three months after the assassination, a most fortuitous event occurred: a Russian named Yuri Nosenko sought political asylum in the United States.

According to CIA records, Nosenko declared that he had been a KGB agent; that in 1959 and again in 1963 he had been assigned to the KGB's American Tourist Section; that in that assignment he had reviewed Oswald's KGB file; and that he could categorically deny that Oswald had in any way been connected with the KGB.

Nosenko's assertions did not end the inquiry into whether Oswald had a KGB connection. In fact, they only tended to complicate it.

This complication arose because some officials of the Central Intelligence Agency expressed doubt that Nosenko was a bona fide defector, which might mean that Nosenko's 'defection' was instead an effort to mislead – a disinformation mission.

According to CIA records, back in 1962, whilst a security escort to a Soviet disarmament delegation in Geneva, Switzerland, Nosenko had offered to sell information to the CIA for 900 Swiss francs, claiming he needed the money to replace KGB funds he had spent on a drinking spree. After his defection he admitted that he had not really needed the money but had felt that an offer to merely give the information away for nothing would be rejected, as had been the case with similar offers by other Soviet agents. (This admission has not received all the study it deserves. For example, how would Nosenko have known of those prior offers, and why was Nosenko supposedly so anxious to pass information to the US as to make up such a story in order to be able to do so?)

Nonetheless, the CIA had made that 1962 deal with Nosenko. According to the records, at that time he asserted that he would never defect because he could never leave his family, and he told the CIA never to contact him in the Soviet Union. However, he assured them that he would make contact the next time he came abroad.

On 23 January 1964, eight weeks after the Kennedy assassination, Nosenko was once again in Geneva as escort to a disarmament delegation. Claiming that he was now disillusioned with his Government, and insisting that he would soon not be able to leave the Soviet Union again, Nosenko declared that he wished to immediately defect.

The CIA stalled, but Nosenko was adamant. Then, 'On 4 February, Nosenko revealed he had received a telegram ordering him to return to Moscow directly. He said he feared the KGB was aware he was working with the West, and his life depended on his being permitted to defect immediately.' Persuaded by his plea, the CIA accepted Nosenko as a defector. Nosenko would later admit that the recall telegram was a fake, and that he had made up the story in order to get the CIA to agree to his defection without further delay.

The FBI, having been informed by the CIA that Nosenko had information about Oswald, interviewed him upon his arrival in the United States. He reiterated what he had told the CIA regarding his knowledge of Oswald, including the reassuring fact that the KGB had never had any contact with President Kennedy's assassin.

The conclusion of the report of this FBI interview reads: 'On 4 March 1964, Nosenko stated that he did not want any publicity in connection with this information but stated he would be willing to testify to this information before the Presidential Commission provided such testimony is given in secret and absolutely no publicity is given either to his appearance before the Commission or to the information itself.' The report also notes that two days later Nosenko inquired if his offer had been given to the appropriate authorities, and he was assured that this had been done.

By April 1964, officials of both the Soviet Russia and the Counter-Intelligence sections of the CIA were raising serious doubts as to whether Nosenko was a bona fide defector. The bases for their misgivings were stated to be that:

(1) Many leads provided by Nosenko had been of the 'giveaway' variety, that is, information that is no longer of significant value to the KGB, or information which in the probable judgement of the KGB is already being probed by Western intelligence, so that there is

more to be gained from having a dispatched agent 'give it away' and thereby gain credibility.

(2) A background check of Nosenko – of his schooling, military career and his activities as an intelligence officer – had led US officials to suspect Nosenko was telling them a 'legend', that is, supplying them with a fabricated identity. Certain aspects of Nosenko's background did not check out, and certain events he described seemed highly unlikely.

(3) Two defectors who had preceded Nosenko were skeptical of him. One was convinced Nosenko was on a KGB mission, the purpose of which was to neutralize information one of the defectors had provided.

(4) Information Nosenko had given about Oswald aroused their suspicions. The chief of the Soviet Russia section had difficulty accepting the statements about Oswald, characterizing them as seeming 'almost to have been tacked on or to have been added, as though it didn't seem to be part of the real body of the other things he had to say, many of which were true'.

On 4 April 1964, the CIA placed Nosenko in isolation and commenced 'hostile interrogations'. The atmosphere was set by conducting a polygraph test wherein the CIA polygrapher was to accuse Nosenko of lying no matter what the test really showed.

Presumably that did not require any great acting ability in this case, for in his report – in which he was to state his true conclusions – the polygrapher declared that Nosenko had indeed lied.

During 1964, Nosenko was interviewed on five occasions wherein at least some questions dealt with Lee Harvey Oswald. His story as it relates to Oswald has been summarized as follows:

'Nosenko related that he was assigned to the Seventh Department of the Second Chief Directorate when Oswald arrived in the Soviet Union in 1959, at which time Nosenko's section had responsibility for counter-intelligence operations against American tourists.

'At the time Oswald asked to remain in Russia, Nosenko reviewed information the KGB had on the American. Soon after Oswald went to Minsk, Nosenko was transferred and lost contact with him. However, he became re-involved in the case right after the assassination.

'Nosenko said that as soon as President Kennedy's assassin was identified as a man who had lived in the Soviet Union, the KGB ordered that Oswald's file be flown to Moscow and reviewed to determine whether there had been any contact between him and Soviet intelligence. Nosenko said further he was assigned to the review of Oswald's file. Based on that review, as well as his earlier contact with the case, he was able to report positively that Oswald had neither been recruited nor contacted by the KGB.'

In October 1966, Nosenko was given his second polygraph test, during which he was again asked about Oswald. The CIA examiner was the same one who had administered the first test and he once again concluded that Nosenko was lying.

The Soviet Russia Section of the CIA wrote a 900-page report based on its interrogations of Nosenko, which was trimmed to 447 pages by the time it was submitted in February 1968. It came to the conclusion that Nosenko:

(1) Did not serve in the naval reserve as he had claimed.

(2) Did not join the KGB at the time or in the manner he described.

(3) Did not serve in the American Embassy section of the KGB at the time he claimed, and was not a senior case officer or deputy chief of the seventh department, as he stated he had been.

(4) Was not chief of the American Embassy section.

(5) Was not a deputy chief of the seventh department in 1962, as he had claimed.

From the time this report was first being drafted, the

thrust of its conclusions was known by, and seemed to create quite a dilemma for, the leadership of the CIA. As a result, in mid-1967 a career security officer was assigned to write a critique of the handling of Nosenko. His conclusion – that Nosenko was who he claimed to be and that he was supplying valid information – led to the official CIA position that Nosenko was a bona fide defector.

On 8 August 1968, Nosenko was given a third polygraph test. Only two of the questions on this test related to information he had supplied about Oswald. This time Nosenko was deemed to have passed the test.

The official position of the CIA relative to the various polygraphs thereupon was stated to be that the third test – the one Nosenko passed – was considered to be a valid test.

As to the first two tests – both of which Nosenko had failed – the official CIA position became that both of those tests were invalid or inconclusive.

In October 1968, the security officer who had been selected by the CIA brass issued a report which disputed each and every conclusion of the report of the Soviet Russia Section written eight months earlier.

However, neither of these reports paid very much attention to the Oswald aspect of the Nosenko case, and neither even attempted to analyze Nosenko's statements about Oswald. The combined total for both reports amounts to 730 pages, only fifteen of which deal in any respect with Oswald.

The security officer's report did, nonetheless, reach the conclusion that Nosenko was not dispatched by the Soviet Government to give false information to the US officials about Oswald. He listed the reasons for this conclusion thus:

(1) Nosenko's first contact with the CIA was in June 1962, 17 months prior to the assassination.

(2) Information provided by Nosenko was not sufficient in 'nature, scope and content' to convince US authorities of no Soviet involvement in the assassination.

(3) Even if the KGB were involved in the assassination, the Soviets would assume that US authorities would, in turn, believe only a few senior officers would be aware of it, and Nosenko would not be one of them.

Amongst the documents obtained by the House Committee is information on finances, in which we learn that:

'Prior to Nosenko's defection on 4 February 1964, he was promised $50,000 for previous cooperation, $10,000 for his identification in 1962 of a particular espionage agent, and $25,000 a year compensation for future services.'

These were not exactly pauper's wages. The average annual earnings of fulltime employees in the US in the year 1964 were $5,503.*

---

* Historical Statistics of the United States, US Department of Commerce, Bureau of the Census, 1975, page 164, Series D 722–727.

BOOK 2

CHAPTER

10

Pick your Polygraph

The House Select Committee undertook its own investigation of the Nosenko case, which involved both the review of existing documentation and the eliciting of new evidence.

As part of its investigation, the Committee retained Richard O. Arther to conduct an independent analysis of Yuri Nosenko's three polygraph tests.

'Arther received a BS with honors in police science from Michigan State University in 1951, and an MA in psychology from Columbia University in 1960. Arther has been in private practice in New York City since 1963. He founded Scientific Lie Detection, Inc. and co-founded the National Training Center of Polygraph Science. He has taught at Brooklyn College, Seton Hall University, the John Jay College of Criminal Justice and the Graduate School of Public Administration of New York University. Arther has authored over 200 professional articles and two books. He is a member of the Academy of Certified Polygraphists and the Amercian Polygraph Association. [. . .]

'A polygraph examination records physiological responses to questions asked. The polygraphist attempts to design the examination in such a way that the truthful person will react to the control questions and the lying person to the relevant questions. The test structure must be constructed so that it poses a threat to both the truthful and untruthful person.

'The polygraphist attempts to determine the "psychological set" of the examinee. He tries to determine, by reading the physiological activity of the examinee in the polygraph charts, what questions or question areas pose the greatest threat to the examinee's well-being. A "psychological set" is a person's fears, anxieties, and apprehension, [which] are channeled toward that situation causing the greatest threat to the individual's well-being. He will tune in on that which is of a greater threat, and tune out that of a lesser threat.

'Responses to questions are recorded on a polygraph chart, which consists of tracings produced by three different types of psychological reactions associated with the circulatory, nervous, and respiratory systems:

(1) The breathing pattern is recorded by means of a rubber tube placed around the person's chest.

(2) The Galvanic skin response is measured by placing the attachments on either the fingers or the palms.

(3) Changes in blood pressure, heart beat, and pulse rate are obtained by a standard blood pressure cuff placed around the upper arm.

'Questions are broken down into three categories:

(1) Relevant – those pertinent to the investigation.

(2) Irrelevant – hopefully, meaningless, non-emotion-producing ones to get the person used to being questioned and giving answers.

(3) Control – non-relevant, to which it can be assumed the person will lie during the test. These provide a standard for comparing the responses to relevant questions.

'If a person reacts more to a proper control question than to the relevant questions, then he is considered to be truthful to the relevants. On the other hand, if he reacts more to the relevants than to the proper control question, he is considered to be lying to the relevants.

'Relevant, irrelevant and control questions are interspersed throughout the polygraph chart. The examination may consist of various series covering various relevant issues. Each relevant issue must be asked a minimum of two times in a series, but as many times as necessary to conclude that relevant issue successfully. Each series should have a minimum of two charts, but, as many charts as necessary to conclude the relevant issues in that series successfully.

'The procedure for a polygraph examination is as follows: The polygraphist first conducts a pre-test interview, during which the test questions are read to the person exactly as they are going to be asked. It is vital that all questions be properly worded and discussed with the person. Then the actual test is conducted.'

Having conducted his independent analysis, Richard O. Arther concluded that the second test – in which the examiner determined Nosenko was lying – was the most valid and reliable of the three examinations administered to Yuri Nosenko.

As for the third test – where the examiner found Nosenko to be telling the truth – Mr Arther, in addressing the only two questions on that exam which related to the information Nosenko had supplied about Oswald, characterized the first such question as 'atrocious' and the second such question as 'very poor' for use in assessing the validity of Nosenko's responses.

The fact is that this third examiner had even found Nosenko to be truthful when he answered 'No' to the question, 'Is there any possibility that the KGB would dispatch an officer to defect to the Americans?'.

BOOK 2

CHAPTER

11

Not Worthy of Belief

The House Select Committee, in considering whether Nosenko was a bona fide defector, was interested to know why the CIA had apparently failed (or refused) to ascertain that there were inconsistencies within Nosenko's various statements, as well as between some of Nosenko's statements and knowledge from other sources.

As part of its investigation on these points, the Committee took the deposition of the CIA employee who interviewed Nosenko on 3 and 27 July 1964. It turned out that this person who the CIA had detailed to question Nosenko, was in no position to challenge Nosenko either on general knowledge or specifically on Oswald. In his deposition this CIA employee told the Committee he was not an expert on the KGB, nor had he any previous experience with KGB defectors. When asked about his knowledge of Oswald, since it was in his interviews that the most detailed questions about Oswald were asked, he replied, 'I cannot specifically recall having read any files pertaining to Lee Harvey Oswald. Certainly I had read and heard a lot about him in the newspapers, television, and radio. I may have had the opportunity to read some previous debriefings of Nosenko concerning Oswald, but I am not sure of that.'

As to the security officer who wrote the 1968 report, when he was asked if he ever spoke to Nosenko about Oswald, he said, 'No. Well, all I have you have there (Nosenko's three page statement). I did a write-up on it. I didn't see that it seriously conflicted with what we had.'

He was then asked, 'And did you ever question him about what he wrote?' To this he responded, 'No, because I had no reason to disbelieve him.'

Questioned further as to why he did not compare all of Nosenko's statements on Oswald, he replied, 'I did not have all the information on the Oswald investigation. That was an FBI investigation.'

The follow-up inquiry was, 'Well, was it available to you if you had asked the FBI for their reports of what Oswald had said to them?' The answer was, 'It might, under certain circumstances, but in this case here, as far as our office was concerned, the Oswald matter was an FBI matter.'

Given the apparent failure of the CIA to critically evaluate the credibility of Nosenko's statements about Oswald, the Committee undertook to do this job, and, in review of all the evidence, the Committee noted that there had been significant inconsistencies over the years in Nosenko's story. A few of these will now be discussed.

In his interviews in 1964, among the points Nosenko stressed was that there had been no physical or technical surveillance on Oswald (in fact, he had even claimed that the KGB did not know that Marina was a friend of Oswald until they applied for marriage because there was no surveillance on Oswald to show that he knew her).

He claimed that he could unequivocally state this because he had thoroughly reviewed Oswald's KGB file. Yet, when being pressed on a slightly different tack in 1978, Nosenko claimed that he had been unable to read the entire Oswald file because it consisted of seven or eight thick volumes of documents due to all the surveillance reports.

Nosenko insisted that the KGB never had any contact whatsoever with Oswald, not even an interview. They not only did not question Oswald when he asked to defect, but they also did not interview him later when it was decided he would be permitted to remain in Russia. At no time did the KGB talk to Oswald.

Yet, when the Committee asked Nosenko, 'Would the KGB have any interest in an American student?', he replied 'As I told you yesterday, the KGB is interested in students, but particularly those students who are studying the Russian language, Russian history, Russian economy.'

A subsequent question began 'Is it your testimony that Lee Harvey Oswald, who was a student, who was a professed Marxist, who had . . .' At this point Nosenko interrupted. 'Students. I never heard that he was a student.'

This is a fascinating statement by a man who claimed to know all there was to know about Oswald in the Soviet Union. Russian documents supplied to the United States presumably from the files Nosenko claimed to have reviewed show that upon his arrival in Moscow Oswald registered at the Hotel Berlin as a 'student'; and in his application for an identity card at the Visa and Registration Office at the Moscow City Council, Oswald had filled out item 13 (occupation) with the word 'student'.

When asked, 'And exactly why did no KGB officer ever speak to Oswald before they made the decision about whether to let him defect?', Nosenko answered, 'We didn't consider him an interesting target.' But, when asked if he knew of any other defector who was turned away because he was uninteresting, Nosenko answered 'No'.

The head of the CIA Soviet Russia Section from 1963

to 1968 was asked by the Committee if he knew of comparable situations in which someone was not questioned, was just left alone, as Nosenko said Oswald was. He replied that he did not know of any former Soviet intelligence officer or other knowledgeable source to whom he had spoken who felt that this would have been possible. 'If someone did,' he said, 'I never heard of it.'

Nosenko was forced to admit that the KGB would have been 'very interested' in the fact that Oswald worked as a radar operator at an air base from which the super secret U-2 spy planes took off and landed. But, Nosenko maintained, the KGB never spoke with Oswald and so it didn't know that he had any connection with the U-2 flights.

As the Committee summarized this tale, 'In short, Nosenko's Oswald story is as follows: The KGB, although very interested in the U-2, never learned anything about it from Oswald because it didn't know he had any knowledge of the aircraft. Why? Because Oswald was never questioned by the KGB because the decision was made that Oswald was of no interest to Soviet intelligence.'

Even John Hart, who appeared before the Committee to support the CIA's assessment that Nosenko was a bona fide defector, had to concede as follows: 'I find it very hard to believe that the KGB had so little interest in this individual. Therefore, if I were in the position of deciding whether to use the testimony of Mr Nosenko on this case or not, I would not use it.'

Mr Hart was asked, '. . .[Y]ou have someone in the Soviet Union who announces he wants to stay, that he wants to live there, that he wants to become a Soviet citizen, and the KGB according to Mr Nosenko decides that on the basis of his application to come to the country he is uninteresting. Now, does that strike you as plausible, based on your information and your knowledge of intelligence and counter-intelligence activities, that the KGB would dismiss that kind of request merely by looking at the entrance applications, and not make an effort to talk to the person, to see what information they might be able to impart?'

The answer to that question by this Nosenko apologist was: 'Congressman, I find it implausible. I might say that if this had ever been the case within the expertise of any of us who had anything to do with Soviet operations, it would have greatly facilitated our tasks in connection with putting people into the Soviet Union . . .'.

Hart's enthusiastic support for Nosenko's bona fides as a defector was rebutted at length by the Deputy Chief, SB Division (a man referred to only as Mr D. C.) who, at the time of Nosenko's first contact with the CIA in Geneva, had served as head of the CIA's section responsible for counter-intelligence against the Soviet intelligence services, and later, as the deputy chief of the Soviet Bloc Division of the CIA, had assisted in further interrogations of Nosenko. As relates to Oswald, the testimony of this witness is dramatic and informative:

'Here was this young American, Lee Harvey Oswald, just out of the Marine Corps, already inside the USSR and going to great lengths to stay there and become a citizen. The KGB never bothered to talk to him, not even once, not even to get an idea whether he might be a CIA plant (and although even Nosenko once said, I think, that the KGB feared he might be). Can this be true?

'Could we all be wrong in what we've heard about rigid Soviet security precautions and about their strict procedures and disciplines, and about how dangerous it is in the USSR for someone to take a risky decison (like failing to screen an applicant for permanent residence in the USSR)? Of course not.'

BOOK 2

CHAPTER

12

A Disinformation Mission?

Having evaluated all of the evidence, the Committee declared, not surprisingly, that they were 'certain Nosenko lied about Oswald'.

However, that still left a question which the Committee could not answer: *Why* did Nosenko lie about Oswald?

As for that issue, all they could do was to observe: 'The reasons he would lie about Oswald range from the possibility that he merely wanted to exaggerate his own importance to the disinformation hypothesis with its sinister implications.'

To this they appended a footnote: 'Beyond those reasons for falsification that can be attributed to Nosenko himself, there has been speculation that the Soviet Government, while not involved in the assassination, sent Nosenko on a mission to allay American fears. Hence, while his story about no connection between Oswald and the KGB might be false, his claim of no Soviet involvement would be truthful.'

The Committee's comments on the question 'Why did Nosenko lie about Oswald?' appear to imply that there is absolutely nothing in the evidence which might prove helpful in trying to answer that question. Perhaps so.

The Committee also appears to be indicating that they have at least set the outer bounds – the range – of the possible answers to that perplexing question. Again, perhaps so.

Yet, careful analysis of the available evidence seems to hint that there may be a very different and perhaps more logical explanation to the Nosenko enigma.

Let us re-examine the known facts and consider if there are reasonable inferences which such facts may warrant.

We are told that Nosenko sold information to the CIA in 1962.

We are later told that Nosenko 'said he feared the KGB was aware he was working with the West, and his life depended on his being permitted to defect immediately'.

Suppose we reword these facts into language more meaningful to our inquiry.

As of 1962, the CIA had compromised Nosenko, and thereby, as of 1962 the CIA 'owned' Nosenko – could at any time force him to do their bidding – because they held over his head the ever present threat of leaking to the Soviets the facts about Nosenko's sale of information to the CIA.

The language ascribed to Nosenko is also informative: 'He said he feared the KGB was aware he *was working* with the West. . .' The tense used hints at something quite to the contrary of the implication in the summary that there had been merely a single contact prior to the time of the defection.

But we need not depend on semantics to show that there had been an ongoing relationship between Nosenko and the CIA. The information in another part of this body of work relative to finances would seem to rather clearly demonstrate that there in fact had been such a relationship:

'Prior to Nosenko's defection on 4 February 1964,

he was promised $50,000 for previous cooperation, $10,000 for his identification, in 1962, of a particular espionage agent, and $25,000 a year for future services.'

In the narrative we are told of only one contact, that being in 1962, and the nature of that contact is said to be the sale of information for the sum of 900 Swiss francs. So, as for the one stated contact, the CIA already had its information and Nosenko already had his money.

For what, then, was the sum of $60,000 being promised, if not for services provided during an ongoing relationship prior to the defection? Indeed, the very language tells us that is just what this $60,000 was for: '$50,000 for previous cooperation', and '$10,000 for his identification, in 1962, of a particular espionage agent'.

So, the evidence would seem to be conclusive that for some period of time preceding his defection, Yuri Nosenko had been a CIA asset – an undercover agent in place – who had been providing valuable services and information to the CIA.

Can there be any question but that under normal circumstances Nosenko's most valuable role to the CIA would be to remain as an agent in place?

Logically, should the CIA want to encourage him to defect, thereby losing a well-placed spy?

Yet, if they were not encouraging him to defect, how else does one explain the statement: *'Prior to Nosenko's defection* on 4 February 1964, *he was promised* $50,000 for previous cooperation, $10,000 for his identification, in 1962, of a particular espionage agent, and $25,000 a year compensation for future services'?

Here was a KGB officer the CIA had 'turned', and over whom they had permanent blackmail privileges. Are we to believe that the soft-hearted CIA let him off the hook just because he wanted out?

No, we are told that he was permitted to defect because he reported that he had received a telegram recalling him immediately to Moscow, and that he feared the Soviets knew he was working with the West, so that his life was in danger if not allowed to defect.

But let's look a bit more closely at this rationalization.

Is there any believable explanation as to why – before allowing this asset, this compromised KGB officer, to defect – no one demanded that he produce the alleged telegram supposedly ordering him back to his death in Moscow?

Here, supposedly, was the proof Nosenko needed to persuade the CIA to permit him to defect. Would anyone have believed it had he said he had destroyed this crucial life-saving evidence? What would he have said: That he destroyed it to keep it a secret? If so, from whom?

We can conclude they never asked for the telegram, since:

(1) We know that no such telegram was sent and so could not have been produced.

(2) Had the telegram been called for, there is no credible excuse Nosenko could have offered for failing to produce it.

It would appear, therefore, that in order to accept the alleged story of Nosenko's defection, we must first accept the premise that in utter dereliction of their duties, the responsible CIA officials permitted a valuable spy, a turned KGB officer, to hornswoggle them into accepting the story of a phantom recall telegram which they never even asked to see, and, in addition, that before permitting him the pleasure of bamboozling them, they first promised him amounts of money which were by 1964 standards most substantial indeed.

The alternative would seem to be that we have not been told a complete and accurate story about Nosenko's defection, which would certainly raise the question as to why we were misled.

All of this leads inexorably to the following questions:

(1) Did the CIA (or elements thereof) order the

defection of the CIA's longtime agent, Yuri Nosenko?

(2) Was it merely a coincidence that Nosenko's defection happened to come at a time when intense scrutiny was being addressed to the background of Lee Harvey Oswald?

(3) By insisting that his testimony about Oswald be given in secret and with absolutely no publicity given, either to his appearance before the Commission or to the information itself, was Nosenko participating in an effort to keep the Russians from knowing that false information was being provided under the cover that it came from them?

Let's follow that last thought for a moment.

Who controlled the input of information if Nosenko's testimony about Oswald had been kept secret from all except those for whose ears it was intended?

What might the investigators be anticipated to suspect when elements of the CIA advise them that Nosenko might be a false defector?

Was Nosenko's Oswald story intentionally designed so that absolutely no one could possibly believe it?

When this possibly false defector relates his blatantly untrue Oswald story, are the listeners expected to conclude that the untrue Oswald story provides the final proof that he was, indeed, a false defector?

When the listeners conclude that this false defector has told an untrue Oswald story, are they to suspect that someone might have sent the false defector?

Are the listeners to suspect that whoever sent the false defector with the untrue Oswald story might have had a reason to want to deflect attention away from some connection they had with Oswald?

Does this mean that it was intended that the investigators should be led to believe that the KGB was trying to deflect attention away from its Oswald connection?

And, finally, if Nosenko was indeed on a disinformation mission, a mission to deflect attention away from an Oswald connection, and if it was not the KGB which sent him, then who sent him and why?

Who Sent Nosenko?

As if there were not already enough twists and turns to
the Nosenko story, there is *possibly* yet another explanation to this increasingly bizarre puzzle. The word
'possibly' is emphasized here because the evidence
upon which this chapter is based was not authenticated
by any of the official investigations we have been
relying upon – at least not directly.

A writer named Edward Jay Epstein, utilizing the
Freedom Of Information Act, obtained documents
detailing the differing CIA perceptions of Yuri
Nosenko, which might best be described as: the
'official' CIA position that he was a bona fide defector;
and the 'contrarian' unofficial view that he was a false
defector.

Mr Epstein's book, *Legend*, was published in 1978,
and it provided to the general public its first real
knowledge of Nosenko. *Legend*, based in good part on
adopting the contrarian view of Nosenko, made out a
strong case that the Russians were seeking to deflect
attention away from some relationship they had with
Lee Harvey Oswald.

As it turns out, during his preparation for the book,

Mr Epstein spoke with the CIA official previously identified as Mr D. C. In his testimony to the House Select Committee, Mr D. C. acknowledged talking with Epstein in that regard, indicating that the primary help he provided to Mr Epstein was to insure that there were no errors in the Nosenko story now being disseminated to the public.

Specifically, Mr D. C. stated in his sworn testimony that while he may not agree with some of the emphasis, '[T]he facts that Mr Epstein has in the book are generally accurate.'

This leads us into yet another labyrinth, for in *Legend* Mr Epstein relates certain facts relating to Yuri Nosenko for which we have no official verification except for this blanket 'Amen' by Mr D. C.

However, these are facts about which Mr D. C. would have firsthand knowledge, and so his endorsement under oath of the accuracy of the facts in Mr Epstein's book is uniquely meaningful. It will be remembered that Mr D. C. has previously been identified as having been in 1962 the head of the CIA's section responsible for counter-intelligence against the Soviet intelligence services. As such, he would have had more than a mere passing interest in a KGB officer who first contacted the Agency in 1962 offering information. More to the point, he testified that he was directly responsible for the case of Yuri Nosenko from 1962 to 1967.

Mr Epstein in his book discloses that at the time of his first meeting with the CIA in 1962, Nosenko had related a story as to how the KGB had come to uncover and execute a CIA 'mole', Pytor Semyonovich Popov.

Popov, a lieutenant colonel in Soviet military intelligence, had for some time been perhaps the highest placed and most valuable CIA spy in Russia. The Agency had an understandable interest in how Popov had come to be discovered, since one obvious possibility which existed was that he had been betrayed by someone on the US side. Nosenko said that Popov had been detected through a new Soviet surveillance technique, which would indicate – comfortingly – that there had been no breach of security within the CIA.

Mr Epstein also discloses that in what would have been late 1958 or early 1959, Richard Bissell, the father of the U-2 spy plane program, told the CIA deputy director of plans, Richard Helms, that Popov had been sending out information that the Russians now had ascertained some specific information about the super secret U-2. This was shocking news, since if they had discovered many of the flight characteristics of the U-2, this could accelerate their ability to design a control system which would permit their high-altitude rockets to knock the planes from the sky. Helms and Bissell wondered how the Soviets could be gaining such knowledge.

Sometime later in 1959, at a meeting in Moscow with his CIA case officer, Popov revealed that the KGB had caught on to him, indicating with hand gestures that he had been wired for sound and passing a note scribbled out on six pages of toilet paper. In September 1959, Popov was arrested and subsequently executed by Soviet counter-intelligence.

Obviously, Nosenko's information that Popov had been caught through a new Soviet surveillance technology would be comforting only if Nosenko were believed. If there were reason to doubt him, it would follow that he might have been sent to deflect attention away from the truth; to wit, that Popov had been identified by a Soviet mole within the American intelligence community.

It is a tribute to their usual tight-mouthed discipline that we laymen tend to view the CIA as a monolithic organization of single-minded people. Spy novels aside, the testimony of and about Yuri Nosenko provides us with a rare glimpse into the real and very human world of the intelligence agent.

We learn, for example, that at the time Nosenko presented himself in 1962, there was an internal struggle within the CIA as to the bona fides of a Russian defector identified as 'X'. Six months earlier, X had defected bringing information that there was a Russian mole highly placed in the American intelligence community. The question arose: Was X sent to sow dissent and distrust in the Agency, or did the intelligence community have the very serious problem of a mole?

The problem becomes more complex. Mr D. C. told the House Select Committee that at the time of Nosenko's initial contact in 1962, he was suspicious of Nosenko because he believed Nosenko was deflecting information which had been given in the previous months by X. In other words, Mr D. C. says that from the word go he believed Nosenko was providing false information in order to deflect American attention away from the information which X had given.

Yet John Hart testified that, 'The first important communication which went back from Geneva after the two American emissaries had met with Mr Yosenko was sent by a man who . . . I am going to call . . . the deputy chief of the SB Division, Soviet Bloc Division, throughout my testimony [elsewhere Hart makes clear that he is referring to the man as the deputy chief of the Soviet Bloc Division although he did not as yet hold that rank]. The deputy chief, who is the chief interrogator over there, sent back a telegram to Washington on 11 June 1962, in which he said "Subject", meaning Nosenko, "has conclusively proved his bona fides. He has provided info of importance and sensitivity. Subject now completely cooperative. Willing to meet when abroad and will meet as often and as long as possible in his departure in Geneva from 15 June."

'On 15 June both Nosenko and the Deputy Chief SB departed from Geneva, Mr Nosenko to return to Moscow and his KGB duties, the Deputy Chief SB to return to Washington.

'In the course of my investigation, I asked the gentleman, who was for many years chief of the CIA counter-intelligence staff, to describe to me what ensued after the arrival in Washington of DCSB, and I shall give you a brief quote which was recorded and transcribed and which is held in our files. This is the chief of the counter-intelligence staff of the CIA speaking:

' "We got the first message from Deputy Chief SB – that is the one I have just previously quoted to you – on Nosenko from Geneva, and Deputy Chief SB was ordered back to Washington, and we had a big meeting here on Saturday morning, and Deputy Chief SB thought he had the biggest fish of his life. I mean he really did. And everything I heard from him, however, was in direct contrast from what we had heard from Mr X".'

In 1978 Mr D.C. told the House Committee, 'In 1962 he made it absolutely clear to us that he would never defect, under no circumstances . . . He not only said he wouldn't defect but he wouldn't accept contact with us inside the Soviet Union. However, he would see us whenever he came out on official duty on Soviet delegations abroad. In January of 1964 he came out and stupefied us with this statement that he now wants to defect.'

We know from previous chapters that this rendition would appear to be incomplete, since the records indicate that there was an ongoing relationship after Nosenko's return to Russia during which he acted as an American agent in place.

In a 1976 internal CIA memorandum, the Chief of the Soviet Russia Division (SR Division) is quoted as stating in a memo dated 10 February 1964, 'First I assured Subject [Mr Nosenko] that I was satisfied that he was genuine. Based on this, and assuming his continued "cooperation" I said we would proceed to make arrangements to bring him to the States. Second, I confirmed our agreement to pay him $25,000 for each year in place ($50,000) plus $10,000 for [a sensitive case] and our readiness to contract for his services at

$25,000 per year. Third, I explained the polygraph he would be expected to take as final proof of his bona fides.'

In a memo dated 17 February 1964, the Chief of the SR Division writes, 'None of the events of the past few days including the way the Soviets played the pre-confrontation publicity or the confrontation itself changes the substance of the conclusions contained in my 10 February memorandum. However, there is greater evidence now I believe for the view that this operation is designed for long-range goals of utmost importance to the Soviets. One of these is probably a massive propaganda assault on CIA in which Subject, most probably as a "re-defected CIA agent", will play a major but not necessarily the sole role.'

We know from previous chapters that from the time of Nosenko's defection, a long and bitter internal battle ensued as to Nosenko's bona fides. And from the material discussed immediately above we can understand that the perceptions of the various CIA factions as to Nosenko were shaped to a great extent by their perception of X.

But what has all this to do with Oswald?

An interesting fact is glossed over in the Nosenko/Oswald summaries of the House Committee. Mr D.C., who was the man on the scene, testified that, 'Nosenko *before* his defection, . . . was meeting us under clandestine circumstances in Geneva. He was telling us about Lee Harvey Oswald. We, of course, took that and got it as straight and as thoroughly as we could under the circumstances. After he defected and came to the United States, it was made clear . . . that the FBI, as the primary investigative agency on the President's assassination, would manage the further and detailed questioning of Mr Nosenko in the United States on his knowledge of Lee Harvey Oswald.'

There is nothing in that rendition to indicate that the FBI was warned at this time that Nosenko's bona fides were in question. Indeed, the conclusion of the FBI report of their interview with Nosenko makes no such reference. Instead, it relates the famous offer by Nosenko to testify before the Warren Commission and the statement that the offer had been passed on to the appropriate authorities. [The records show that at a later date J. Edgar Hoover expressed himself as believing that Nosenko was a valid defector but that Mr X was a provocateur].

It would appear from the official summaries that – only after the Warren Commission had been briefed on Nosenko's story that Oswald had never been contacted by the KGB – the CIA met informally with Commission member Allen Dulles to inform him that Nosenko's bona fides were in doubt.

The official summaries imply that the doubts began after the Commission had been told Nosenko's Oswald story. However, the testimony of Mr D.C. contradicts that, and indeed, indicates that the doubts went back to the time of the 1962 contact.

Whatever the truth on these matters, the result is the same:The Warren Commission received information which could only lead them to suspect an Oswald/KGB connection, thereby deflecting them from considering any other possible connection.

For a period of time after his defection, the monies promised to Nosenko before his defection were not paid. Obviously, whether the challenges to his bona fides were sincere or a sham, it wouldn't do to be paying him monies at that time. By the late 60s, the money had been worked out, and by the time of the House hearings in 1978, Nosenko was receiving in excess of $35,000 per year as a 'consultant'.

In a memorandum to the Director of Central Intelligence dated 5 October 1972, Harold J. Osborn, Director of Security, states: 'An analysis of this case clearly indicates that Mr Nosenko has been an extremely valuable source, one who has identified many hundreds of Soviet Intelligence Officers, and he has otherwise provided a considerable quantity of useful information on the organization of the KGB, its operational doctrine, and methods. [Sensitive info has] been forwarded to the Federal Bureau of Investigation based on data from Mr Nosenko. He has conducted numerous special security reviews on Soviet subjects of specific intelligence interest, and he has proven himself to be invaluable in exploring counter-intelligence leads. He recently authored a book which is of interest to the Agency. In effect, Mr Nosenko has shown himself to be a productive and hardworking defector, who is "rehabilitated" and favorably disposed towards the Agency.'

Then, in 1978, the House Committee received testimony by and about Nosenko which could only cause them to suspect an Oswald/KGB connection, thus deflecting them also from even considering some other possible connection. The question arises: How or why is it that this 'extremely valuable' CIA employee delivers testimony about Oswald which the CIA then disowns as implausible and incredible?

After Nosenko again asserted he could state positively that Soviet intelligence had had no interest in ex-Marine Oswald because they didn't think he was interesting, a CIA official named David Murphy made sure everyone understood that was nonsense: 'They will talk to a marine about close order drill. You follow me? It doesn't require that he be known to have been a radar operator or a . . . they would talk to him about his military affiliations just as we would . . . We in Germany will talk to a private in the East German Border Guards, period. The GRU would be interested in talking to a private. He was a corporal in the Marine Corps, who had stated to a consul in a consular office, which is manned by the Soviets, Soviet locals and what have you, fully accessible to the Soviets, unlike the higher floors of the Embassy, that he wanted to talk about his experiences, that he wanted to tell all. I guess I found it difficult to believe; this is one of the things that made (or one of the things that created) an atmosphere of disbelief: that there must be something to this case that is important, vitally important to the Soviet Union, and we can't understand it.'

CIA Director Richard Helms, while on the one hand supporting Nosenko's bona fides as a defector, left no room for doubt in his testimony that the Committee should disbelieve Nosenko on Oswald.

In response to the question, 'Given your work in the whole field of intelligence, is it reasonable for this Committee to assume that with Oswald's background and his attempt to defect, that he would be an "uninteresting target" to the KGB?', Richard Helms testified, 'I simply do not understand that assertion. I would have thought, to begin with, that any American who went to the Russian Government and said "I want to defect to the Soviet Union" would have immediately been taken over by the KGB to find out what his game was because, after all, the KGB's charter is to protect the Soviet state against infiltration.

'How would they know that he was serious about this? How would they know that the CIA had not sent him to make a fake defection and to try to get into Soviet society through this device? So for that reason, if not for many others, I find it quite incredible, the assertion by Nosenko that Oswald was never interrogated or was never in touch with the KGB while he was in the Soviet Union. This really stretches one's credulity. It goes back to the testimony this morning that this is the hardest thing about the whole Nosenko case to swallow, and I have not been able to swallow it in all these years.'

The morning testimony to which Helms was referring began with a question by Chairman Stokes: 'If it were clearly proven that Nosenko's statements concerning Oswald were untrue, what significance would you attach to such a finding insofar as the broader question of his overall bona fides are concerned?'

To which Helms replied, 'I think, Mr Stokes, that is just the point. This is the issue which remains, as I understand it, to this very day, that no person familiar with the facts, of whom I am aware, finds Mr Nosenko's comments about Lee Harvey Oswald and the KGB to be credible. That still hangs in the air like an incubus. I think, therefore, this tends to sour a great deal of one's opinion of all the other things he may have contributed to the knowledge of the intelligence community about Soviet affairs and Soviet agents and so forth.

'I do not know how one resolves this bone in the throat. And therefore, if I sit here before you and say, Mr Stokes, I believe that Mr Nosenko is a bona fide defector and you can rely on everything he says, I am in effect saying now, Mr Stokes, you can rely on what he says about Lee Harvey Oswald. And I would not like to make that recommendation to you. That is where this thing lies and it is a most difficult question even at this late date.'

The true culmination of all this came a little further on, when Chairman Stokes asked: 'So it leaves you with the conclusion, then, that if Nosenko was lying about Oswald, that Oswald would in fact be left as being an agent of the KGB?', to which Helms responded 'By implication'.

It would seem more accurate to say: If Nosenko was lying about Oswald, then, by implication, Oswald would be left as being the agent of whoever sent Nosenko.

BOOK 2

CHAPTER

14

The Agency

In 1964, the CIA advised the Warren Commission that the Agency had never had a relationship of any kind with Lee Harvey Oswald. CIA Director John A. McCone testified not only that Oswald was not an agent, employee, informant of the CIA, and was never associated or connected directly or indirectly in any way whatsoever with the Agency, but, further, he swore that:

'The Agency never contacted him, interviewed him, talked with him, or solicited any reports or information from him, or communicated with him directly or in any other manner.'

Does this sound strikingly like what Nosenko said as regards the KGB and Oswald? Is it any more believable?

Is it believable that the CIA, which routinely attempts to solicit information from Americans traveling to Russia, would not even contact and attempt to debrief a returning defector who had lived in Russia for some two and a half years?

Let us accept that, for whatever reason, it is believable.

Is it believable if we consider the interest the CIA would clearly have – if not in this particular defector, as such – in adding to their information as to how the Russians handle defectors, should they want to 'plant' a defector?

Is it still believable if we now add the following additional facts?

(1) The returning defector had been a Marine radar operator carrying a security clearance of 'Confidential'

(2) He had worked at an air base where the super secret U-2 spy plane took off and landed

(3) Since his defection, Francis Gary Powers had been shot down over Russia in the first ever successful downing of a U-2.

Let us now add another little-known, but vital fact to the inquiry we have just begun.

It has been reported in passing that during his years in the Soviet Union, Oswald worked in the Belorussian Radio and Television Factory in Minsk.

It so happens that the CIA had a very great interest in this particular radio factory. They actively collected and carefully accumulated reams of information on the plant, and there were volumes of documents on the facility maintained in the Office of Research and Reports.

Given the CIA's interest in this particular radio factory, is it believable that the CIA would not even attempt to debrief Oswald when he re-defected?

What are we to make of this categorical denial by the CIA that they ever had even the slightest contact with Oswald?

Let us look more carefully at this new piece of information, and see if it might tie in with any knowledge we learned earlier.

To do that, let's explore two seemingly unrelated questions and see if there may be some point of convergence between them.

(1) Why was the CIA so interested in the Minsk radio factory?

(2) How did the Russians come to assign Oswald to this facility?

Since neither the CIA nor the Russians have been forthcoming with answers to these questions, we must approach the issue from a somewhat different tack.

Are we to assume that the CIA's interest in this plant was because they were concerned that the Russians were about to swamp American markets with Russian radios or TVs?

Or, is it more logical to ask if there might have been some military implications to some of the activities at the Minsk radio plant?

What type of activities might take place at a radio plant that might have military implications?

Let's return to a topic we discussed much earlier.

Radio waves are used in a very important system which has significant military implications. By definition, radar is 'a method of detecting distant objects and determining their position, velocity, or other characteristics by analysis of very high frequency radio waves reflected from their surfaces'.

Surely, if the Russians were doing some radar work at this plant, that fact would seem to provide an answer to both of the questions we are currently exploring. It would explain the CIA's interest in the plant, and it would explain why the Russians sent Oswald there.

But where does that lead us?

We know from the testimony of John Hart that the CIA had, as part of its operations, the task of 'putting people into the Soviet Union'. Why would they want to infiltrate people into the Soviet Union?

Is it reasonable to assume that the CIA did not on mere whim expose people to the great physical risk of 'putting them into the Soviet Union'? Is it reasonable to assume that such risks were undertaken only in order to procure specific information which second-hand reports could not adequately provide?

Let us take as a given the great interest the CIA had in this plant, together with the presumption that they must have had a good reason for that interest – for example, radar. Let us then assume hypothetically that the CIA desired to put their own man into that plant.

How might they go about infiltrating this spy into the plant?

Well, if the reason for the CIA interest was Russian radar work at that plant, it may seem a good bet that if the Russians had an American defector who was a radar operator, they might wish to utilize his knowledge at the Minsk plant.

Of course, for that to happen, the CIA's man must be a radar operator – regardless of whether he really has the aptitude for that specialty or not.

If, for example, the man selected had on his aptitude tests scored significantly below the average in arithmetic and pattern code analysis, that would not deter from his being assigned to radar, since the radar assignment would be not because of his aptitude, but because of his future mission.

And if he finished his first six-week radar course forty-sixth in a class of fifty-four, that was no reason to drop him from the specialty.

All that was needed was to help him place seventh in the class of thirty who went on to the second six-week radar course.

So, in our hypothesis, we now have ourselves Lee Harvey Oswald, radar operator. But we need more. We need a radar operator who will be accepted as a bona fide defector.

There happens to be an interesting thing about this Oswald. Within the recent past, preceding his entry to the Marines, he has been demonstrating an interest in socialism and communism.

And, since entering the service, this Oswald has

become more and more blatant in overtly showcasing his interest in things Russian, to the point where his fellow Marines call him 'Oswaldskovich', apparently to his pleasure. He has his name written in Russian on one of his jackets; he plays records of Russian songs 'so loud that one could hear them outside the barracks'; he frequently makes remarks in Russian, and uses expressions like 'da' and 'nyet' and addresses others and is addressed as 'Comrade'; he has been known to have come over and said jokingly, 'You called?' when one of his fellow Marines plays a particular record of Russian music; he makes a point of expressing a preference for the red pieces in chess, forming the 'Red Army'; he regularly and openly reads a Russian language newspaper; and he is openly studying the Russian language.

Certainly, the last place one would wish to station such a Marine with this great vulnerability to things Russian, would be at Atsugi Air Base in Japan, near which there is known to be operating a KGB program aimed at recruiting US military personnel.

Not that one need worry that the Russians would encourage Oswald to defect. They, as assuredly as the CIA, would want a new asset to remain in place as an undercover agent – a spy.

However, contact with this KGB program, together with a history of being a malcontent as evidenced by two court martials, might be persuasive items on his résumé at a later point.

Despite the claim by CIA officials that it was possible Oswald had been recruited by the KGB during his military tour of duty overseas, it is more logical to presume that had he truly been recruited there, the Russians would not have wanted him to defect for the reasons stated above. However, if they did want him to defect, they surely would not have needed to send him halfway around the world to Gregory Golub in Helsinki, Finland – only a narrow body of water separates Japan from Russia. Nor would Oswald or the Russians have been much concerned with the niceties of his finishing his enlistment if he were a true defector.

Is there any more logical explanation for Oswald's trek from New Orleans to Le Havre to London to Helsinki than that someone directed him to Gregory Golub, who could get him an entry visa without prior approval of Moscow?

Who was that? It surely wasn't the Russians. If they wanted Oswald in Russia, they did not need to send him to someone who could get him in without prior approval. Moreover, we know that Oswald was neither expected nor welcomed in Moscow, as evidenced by his reception – or lack thereof – when he arrived.

On the other hand, if the CIA had their radar operator whom they wished to clandestinely infiltrate into the Soviet Union, how better could they attempt to 'put him into the Soviet Union' than by directing him to Gregory Golub, who was not only known to have authority to issue entry visas without prior Moscow approval, but also was known to have exercised that right without prior investigation?

A former CIA finance officer named James Wilcott provided the House Select Committee on Assassinations with information that Lee Harvey Oswald had been a CIA agent who had received financial disbursements under an assigned cryptonym (a code designation for an agency project) and that he himself had disbursed payments for Oswald's project. In the face of categorical denials by every other CIA witness and the absence of any documentation to the contrary, the Committee concluded that Wilcott's allegation was not worthy of belief.

The Committee also had testimony from CIA personnel that a review of Agency files would not always indicate whether an individual was affiliated with the Agency in any capacity. And they recognized that there was not always an independent means of verifying that all materials requested from the Agency had, in fact, been provided. The Committee acknowledged that the very institutional characteristics that are designed to prevent penetration by foreign powers (such as the Agency's strict compartmentalization and the complexity of its enormous filing system) have the simultaneous effect of making congressional inquiry difficult.

Accordingly, the Committee specifically pointed out that, 'Any finding that is essentially negative in nature – such as that Lee Harvey Oswald was neither associated with the CIA in any way, nor ever in contact with that institution – should explicitly acknowledge the possibility of oversight.'

There are certain things that must be analyzed which are relevant to the question of whether Oswald was a true defector or an American agent.

As of October 1959, the State Department had information which should have caused it to prepare a 'lookout card' for Lee Harvey Oswald. A lookout card was filed in the lookout file in the Passport Office, and whenever anyone applied for a passport from any city in the world, his application was immediately forwarded to this office and his name and date of birth checked against the lookout file and if a lookout card was filed, appropriate action, including the possible refusal of a passport, was taken. No such lookout card pertaining to Lee Harvey Oswald was ever located and the Warren Commission reported that 'certain file entries indicate that such card was never prepared'.

In itself, the absence of a lookout card may prove little. However, as part of a mosaic of oddities, it may take on some meaning.

Since long before the time we are discussing, the CIA has maintained what are known as 201 files. '201 files are opened when a person is considered to be of potential intelligence or counter-intelligence significance. The opening of such a file is designed to serve the purpose of placing certain CIA information pertaining to that individual in one centralized records system. The 201 file is maintained in a folder belonging to the Directorate for Operations, the Agency component responsible for clandestine activities.'

A confidential State Department telegram dated 31 October 1959, sent from Moscow to Washington and forwarded to the CIA, reported that Oswald, a recently discharged Marine, had appeared at the US Embassy in Moscow to renounce his American citizenship and 'has offered Soviets any information he has acquired as [an] enlisted radar operator'. At least three other communications of a confidential nature that gave more detail on the Oswald case were sent to the CIA in about the same time period. Agency officials questioned by the Committee testified that the substance of the 31 October 1959 cable was sufficiently important to warrant the opening of a 201 file. Oswald's file, however, was not opened until 9 December 1960.

An Agency memorandum dated 18 September 1975 indicates that Oswald's file was opened on 9 December 1960 in response to the receipt of five documents: two from the FBI, two from the State Department and one from the Navy. This explanation, however, is inconsistent with the presence in Oswald's file of four State Department documents dated in 1959 and a fifth dated 25 May 1960.

The 18 September 1975 memo also states that Oswald's file was opened on 9 December 1960 as a result of his 'defection' to the USSR on 31 October 1959 and renewed interest in Oswald brought about by his queries concerning possible re-entry into the United States. There is no official indication, however, that Oswald expressed to any US Government official an intention to return to the United States until mid-February 1961 (although there is the statement in Oswald's letter – inconsistent with his diary – stating it was a 'second request'). The Committee interviewed a number of Agency people who attempted to explain away the above situation. The Committee, even after accepting their analysis of what had happened, declared, 'Even so, this analysis only explained why a file on Oswald was finally opened; it did not explain the seemingly long delay in the opening of the file.'

The form used to initiate the opening of a 201 file contains a box entitled 'Other Identification'. Lee Harvey Oswald's form had in that box the designation 'AG'. The Agency's explanation of this designation was that AG was a code meaning 'actual or potential defectors to the East or the Sino/Soviet block including Cuba'. Unfortunately, no one on the Committee asked why the CIA would need a secret code on their internal records to denote that the subject had defected or might defect: why not just enter 'defector' or 'potential defector'? Confusingly, another CIA witness said the 'A' represented Communism while the 'G' would represent some category within the Communist structure. All the Agency witnesses were most adamant that the one thing that AG did not stand for was AGency.

The form used to initiate the opening of Oswald's 201 file contains a notation that this file was to be 'restricted'. The CIA admittedly had a practice of restricting access to agents' files to persons on a 'need-to-know' basis. This restriction meant that any person seeking access to the file would first have to notify the restricting officer. The explanation offered by the CIA on this restriction was that the restricting officer had done so simply to allow her to remain aware of any developments that might have occurred with regard to the file. However, no explanation was offered as to why this was necessary. Obviously, if the usual practice was for the person opening the file to be kept abreast of developments, there would be no need to mark a file 'restricted' in order to kick the file back to her.

At the time Oswald was in the Soviet Union, the CIA had a program known as 'HT-Lingual', the purpose of which was to obtain intelligence and counter-intelligence information from letters sent between the United States and Russia. Intercepted letters and envelopes would be photographed and then returned to the mails.

Despite the fact that Oswald was known to have sent or received more than fifty communications during his stay in the Soviet Union, the CIA represented that they had only one letter in their possession directly related to Oswald, a letter dated 6 July 1961 sent by Marguerite Oswald. The Committee, having questioned why the Agency ostensibly had just this one Oswald letter, stated, 'In essence, the Agency's response suggested that HT-Lingual only operated 4 days a week, and, even then, proceeded on a sampling basis.'

The Committee's review of HT-Lingual files pertaining to the Oswald case resulted in the discovery amongst other things of a reproduction of an index card regarding Lee Harvey Oswald dated 9 November 1959, which stated that Oswald was a recent defector to the USSR and a former Marine. It also bears the notation 'CI/Project/RE' and some handwritten notes.

The Committee questioned former employees of the CIA who may have had some knowledge pertaining to the HT-Lingual project in general and this card in particular. Some of these employees recognized the card as relating to the HT-Lingual project, but were unable to identify the meaning of the notation 'CI/Project/RE'. However, one employee testified that the 'CI/Project' was 'simply a name of convenience that was used to describe the HT-Lingual project'. Another testified that 'CI/Project' was the name of the component that ran the HT-Lingual project, and that 'RE' represented the initials of a person who had been a translator of foreign language documents.

The Agency's explanation for the term 'CI/Project/RE' was that there existed an office within the counter-intelligence staff that was known as 'CI/Project', a cover title that had been used to hide the true nature of the office's function of exploiting the material produced by the HT-Lingual project, and that RE represented the initials of a former employee. Thus, the Agency said, the full meaning of the notation was that on 9 November 1959, an employee whose initials were RE placed Oswald's name on the 'watch list' for the HT-Lingual project for the reason stated on the card: that Oswald was a recent defector to the USSR and a former Marine.

The Agency's response also offered explanations for the handwritten material on the card, which was the number '7–305', and the notation 'N/R–RI,20 Nov.59'.

The number 7–305, they said, was a reference to the communication from the CI staff to the Office of Security expressing the CI staff's interest in seeing any mail to or from Oswald in the Soviet Union.

The notation 'N/R–RI,20 Nov.59', according to the Agency, signified that a name trace run through the central records register indicated that there was no record for Lee Oswald as of that date.

How do these explanations of the Agency stand up to examination? Let's start at the end.

They claim that 'N/R–RI,20 Nov.59' signifies that a name trace run through the central records register indicated that there was no record for Lee Oswald as of that date. Yet, that is in direct conflict with other Agency records which indicate the receipt of a telegram concerning Oswald on 31 October 1959, and of two telegrams from the Navy concerning him on 3 and 4 November 1959.

They claim that the handwritten number 7–305 is a reference to the communication from the CI staff to the Office of Security expressing the CI staff's interest in seeing *any* mail to or from Oswald in the Soviet Union. Is this supposed to mean that the picking up of Oswald's letters is not to be left to chance (sampling)? But how does this square with the Agency's position that they have only one of the more than fifty communications to or from Oswald? Does it mean that the Office of Security is being advised that any Oswald communications which do happen to be picked up should be forwarded to the CI staff?

Wouldn't that then make it rather superfluous for RE to also note that Oswald's name be placed on a watch list for the HT-Lingual Project, which is the Agency's explanation for the entry CI/Project/RE?

One aspect of that explanation which deserves more thought is the Agency's interpretation of 'CI/Project'. They say there was an office within the counter-intelligence staff that was known as CI/Project, a cover title that had been used to hide the true nature of the office's functions; and further they say that in fact this office was responsible for the exploitation of the material produced by the HT-Lingual project.

That sounds good if you say it fast. But when you say it slow and consider what you are saying, certain questions emerge. For example, what would be the purpose of having the HT-Lingual project at all unless you were going to exploit the material it produced? If we take as a given that all the material is being gathered in the expectation of being exploited, doesn't it follow that all the material being produced would be of interest to the office responsible for exploiting the material? So, why would this particular card have on it a notation 'CI/Project', supposedly identifying the exploitation unit?

Two Agency employees gave slightly different explanations for CI/Project, one stating that this was a name of convenience to describe the HT-Lingual project, and the other that it was the name of the component that ran the HT-Lingual project. To these explanations, the comments in the preceding paragraph might with equal force be made, and, in addition, it may well be asked why the code name HT-Lingual had been invented if it was going to need yet another code name, CI/Project, to refer to it?

Richard E. Snyder, it will be remembered, was the consular official in the US Embassy in Moscow who had handled the Oswald case both in 1959 at the time of the defection, and in 1961 at the time the re-defection was initiated. It so happens that during 1949–50, while awaiting his foreign service appointment with the State Department, Snyder had worked for the CIA. However, Snyder swore to the Committee, he had had no contact with the CIA since resigning from the Agency in March 1950, other than a letter written in 1970 or 1971 inquiring about employment on a contractual basis.

The Committee found that Snyder's CIA file revealed that at one time prior to 1974 it had been red flagged and maintained on a segregated basis. The file contained a routing indicator that stated that the file had been red flagged because of a 'DCI (Director of Central Intelligence) statement and a matter of cover' concerning Snyder. In response to a Committee inquiry, the CIA indicated that the DCI statement presumably refered to comments which former Director Richard Helms had made in 1964 concerning the Oswald case (which was then under intense study) when Helms was Deputy Director for Plans. The CIA also stated that Snyder's file had been flagged at the request of DDO/CI (Directorate of Operations/Central Intelligence) to insure that all inquiries concerning Snyder would be referred to that office. The Agency was unable to explain the reference to 'cover' because according to its records Snyder had never been assigned any cover while employed. Further, the Agency stated that 'There is no record in Snyder's official personnel file that he ever worked, directly or indirectly, in any capacity for the CIA after his resignation on 26 September 1950' (he had said March).

The Committee did not regard this explanation as satisfactory, especially since Snyder's 201 file indicated that for approximately one year during 1956–7 he had been used by an Agency case officer as a spotter at a university campus because of his access to others who might be going to the Soviet Union, nor was the Agency able to explain specifically why someone considered it necessary to red flag the Snyder file.

Knowing that Snyder may have had a CIA role while in Moscow, when combined with the fact that it was common knowledge that the Russians had hundreds of bugs in the Embassy, gives rise to the intriguing possibility that Snyder and Oswald were engaging in a charade for the benefit of eavesdropping Russian ears, when Oswald went to the Embassy to announce that he had important information he was going to give to the Russians. There can be no question that that act (together with the newspaper interest in Oswald, which was also initiated by Snyder) got some action from the Russians, who had been cautious about Oswald to that point.

Shortly after Lee Oswald had married Marina at the end of April 1961, a Dr Alexis H. Davidson began a tour of duty as the US Embassy physician in Moscow. Davidson stated to the Committee that in connection with this assignment, he had received some 'superficial' intelligence training. This training, he said, mainly involved lectures on Soviet life and instructions on remembering and reporting Soviet names and military activities.

For reasons which will be immediately made clear, Davidson could not have attempted to claim total naiveté with respect to intelligence matters. And perhaps his training was not quite so 'superficial' as he claimed.

The fact is that for at least a year during his Moscow tour of duty, Davidson served as part of the signal system for a CIA agent who was a highly placed GRU officer, Colonel Oleg Penkovsky. When the Soviets finally broke the Penkovsky case in 1963, Davidson was publicly declared *persona non grata.*

Meanwhile, back in 1961 and 1962, while Davidson was still on duty in Moscow, Lee Harvey Oswald was in the process of beginning his re-defection. What, if any, relationship this physician/agent had with Lee Harvey Oswald has never been ascertained.

However, after the assassination of President Kennedy, it was discovered that the name of Dr Davidson's mother and her address in Atlanta, Georgia were in Oswald's address book under the heading 'Mother of US Embassy Doctor'. In addition, it was determined that the flight that the returning Oswalds took from New York to Dallas on 14 June 1962 had stopped in Atlanta.

BOOK 3

THE INTELLIGENCE CONNECTION

BOOK 3

CHAPTER

15

The Aristocratic Spy

Upon his return from Russia in June 1962, Oswald and his family lived for several months in Fort Worth, Texas. In October, Lee went alone to Dallas, got a job, and at the beginning of November moved his wife and daughter to Dallas.

They remained in the Dallas area until April 1963, when Lee moved to New Orleans, leaving his wife and daughter in Irving, a suburb of Dallas, at the home of Ruth Paine, whom they had first met in February.

His little family rejoined Lee in mid-May and they resided together in New Orleans until 22 September when Marina (who was eight months pregnant) and June returned to live at Ruth Paine's. They remained at Ruth Paine's even after Lee moved back to Dallas on 3 October; and, though Lee visited from time to time, it was at Ruth Paine's that Marina was living on 20 October, when she gave birth to their second daughter, Rachel; and it was at Ruth Paine's that she was residing with their children on 22 November 1963.

From the time of their arrival from Russia, Lee and Marina had become acquainted with the growing number of people of the Russian-speaking community in the Dallas–Fort Worth area, who were attracted to each other by a common background, language and culture. With just one exception, Lee himself appears to have had only short-lived contacts with these people.

The exception, George de Mohrenschildt, was more than just a close friend; he was also a man for whom Oswald had appreciable respect.

De Mohrenschildt had an impressive pedigree. Amongst his ancestors was Baron Hilienfelt, a Baltic Swede who fought in the American Army of Independence; and an uncle, Ferdinand de Mohrenschildt, had been First Secretary of the last Russian Embassy in Washington under the Czarist Government.

His father, Sergius Alexander von Mohrenschildt, a 'marshall of nobility' in Minsk Province, had served as director of the Nobel interests in Czarist Russia. Following the Revolution, Sergius was jailed several times by the Communist regime and then was banished for life to Siberia, from where he escaped with his family to Poland.

George's brother, Dimitri, had served in the Czarist Russian Imperial Navy. After the Revolution he joined anti-Communist groups for which he was jailed by the Communists and sentenced to death. Released in a prisoner exchange, Dimitri had emigrated to the United States in 1920 where he remained a 'ferocious anti-Communist'.

George had been about ten years of age when he fled with his parents from Russia to Poland. After attending a Polish cavalry military academy, he studied in Antwerp and attended the University of Liège from which he received a doctor's degree in international commerce in 1928.

In 1938, he emigrated to the United States, where he went to to work as a salesman for the Shumaker Co. in New York. The chief of export for the Shumaker Co., Pierre Fraiss, soon became one of de Mohrenschildt's best friends. Fraiss was connected with French intelligence, and before long de Mohrenschildt was working for Fraiss collecting facts on people involved in pro-German activities. This intelligence work for Fraiss took him around the United States.

It also involved contacting oil companies in the United States about selling oil to the French in competition against German oil supplies during the war. In 1944 de Mohrenschildt entered the University of Texas, from where he received a master's degree in petroleum geology and petroleum engineering in 1945. From that time on he became active as a petroleum engineer throughout the world.

It appears, though, that petroleum engineering may not have been all he was doing throughout the world.

For example, following his trip in 1957 to Yugoslavia for the International Cooperation Administration, de Mohrenschildt was debriefed on that country on several occasions by the CIA in the person of their agent J. Walton Moore.

There were a number of further contacts between Moore and de Mohrenschildt for debriefing purposes during the ensuing years, at which some of the subjects discussed included China and Latin America. Interestingly enough, de Mohrenschildt told the Warren Commission that he 'asked Moore and Ft. Worth attorney Max Clark about Oswald to reassure himself that it was "safe" for the de Mohrenschildts to assist Oswald. According to his testimony, de Mohrenschildt was told by one of the persons he talked to about Oswald, although he said he could not remember who it was, that "the guy seems to be OK".' Since there is no indication who Clark was or whether he had any contact at all with Oswald, the question arises as to what basis CIA agent Moore might have had for giving the 'OK' to this returned defector.

By 'happenstance', at the time of the Bay of Pigs invasion de Mohrenschildt was in Guatemala City, the control center of the CIA's multi-million dollar invasion preparation operation.

One of de Mohrenschildt's world-wide contacts was

with Clemard Joseph Charles, President of the Banque Commerciale d'Haiti. In early May 1963, Charles began a visit to the United States. Colonel Sam Kail, an Army Intelligence officer who was working in Miami, contacted Dorothe Matlack of the office of the Army Chief of Staff for Intelligence. The work of Mrs Matlack, who served as Assistant Director of the Office of Intelligence of the Army, included 'human source collection of intelligence' and involved serving in a liaison capacity with the Central Intelligence Agency. Colonel Kail suggested that Mrs Matlack talk to Charles when he visited Washington, DC, because of Charles' relationship to President Duvalier of Haiti and Haiti's strategic position relative to Cuba.

On 7 May 1963, Mrs Matlack met in the Capitol with Charles and de Mohrenschildt, apparently after having first made hotel reservations for them. Because of the potential political information Charles could give about the current situation in Haiti, she decided that the CIA should become the primary contact with Charles, and so she also arranged for Charles to meet with Tony Czaikowski of the CIA, whom she introduced as a professor from Georgetown University.

The House Select Committee related that, 'A *Washington Post* article by Norman Gale, dated 29 September 1964, reported that Haitian President François Duvalier had received two T-28 fighter planes from Dallas, Texas. The article stated the planes were flown to Haiti illegally. According to the article, Duvalier made down payment on the planes with a letter of credit drawn on the Banque Commerciale of Port-au-Prince, Haiti. The article identified Clemard Joseph Charles as president and principal stockholder of the bank and a close ally of Duvalier. The article stated that Charles visited the United States earlier in 1964 to buy boats and other weapons, and that he visited Dallas during that trip.'[. . .]

'In an airgram dated 2 May 1967 from the Department of State to the American Embassy at Port-au-

Prince, Haiti, it was reported that a man named Edward Browder had leased a plane for one year starting on 24 November 1964 in the name of a phony company and had flown the plane to Port-au-Prince and left it there. The airgram reported also that Browder later cashed a check for $24,000 signed by Clemard Joseph Charles. Another airgram from the State Department to the Embassy dated 25 May 1967 verified that the check to Browder was drawn from the personal account of Clemard Joseph Charles at Manufacturers Hanover Trust Bank.

'Edward Browder was interviewed by the Committee at the Federal Penitentiary at MacNeill Island, Washington, where he was serving a 25-year sentence for securities violations. During his interview, Browder discussed a series of gun-running and smuggling operations he was involved in during the 1960s that were intended to result in the eventual overthrow or assassination of Fidel Castro. Browder stated that this work included assistance by the CIA in the form of money and operations. Browder said that during that period he did purchase at least two B-25 planes to be used in "smuggling operations" which would be used to assist the gun-running and raids against Cuba.'

The House Committee interviewed Joseph Dryer, a Palm Beach, Florida, stockbroker who, they had learned, had known George de Mohrenschildt in Haiti. According to Dryer, during the 1950s and 60s, he, Clemard Joseph Charles, and George de Mohrenschildt were associated with a woman named Jacqueline Lancelot, who owned a well-known restaurant in Petionville, Haiti. Dryer said the restaurant was frequented by many American intelligence personnel from the American Embassy, and other foreigners. Lancelot, he said, had contact with the American intelligence operatives and passed them information about the Duvalier government. Dryer said that his relationship with Lancelot included passing messages for her to people in the United States whom Dryer assumed were connected in some way to the CIA.

Dryer also told the Committee the following bit of hearsay information. He said that Lancelot had told him shortly after the Kennedy assassination that a 'substantial' sum of money, $200,000 or $250,000, had been deposited in de Mohrenschildt's account in a Port-au-Prince bank (not Charles' bank). According to Dryer, Lancelot said her source of information was the person who handed out the funds at the bank; that the money was subsequently paid out, although she did not know to whom; and de Mohrenschildt left Haiti soon after.

Given this hint at George de Mohrenschildt's fascinating and exciting exploits over the years, his 1962–3 friendship with Lee Harvey Oswald surely made for a rather strange pairing, to say the least. De Mohrenschildt, sophisticated and well educated, was a man who moved easily in the social and professional circles of wealthy Texas oilmen and the so-called 'White Russian' community in Dallas, many of whom were avowed right-wingers. Oswald, because of his 'lowly' background which did not include much education or influence, and because of his Marxist ideological positions, was shunned by most of the people de Mohrenschildt counted among his friends.

When Oswald first moved to Dallas on 9 October 1962, before he even established a residence, he opened a post office box (#2915) at the Dallas General Post Office. His application for the box listed his address as that of George de Mohrenschildt's daughter, Alexandra de Mohrenschildt Taylor.

Finally, there is this intriguing 'teaser' of the George de Mohrenschildt story. It appears that de Mohrenschildt had some type of association with a man named William Avery Hyde. This is, an intriguing teaser because Hyde just happened to be the father of Ruth Paine, the woman with whom Marina and the children were permanently residing after September 1963.

And on 14 October 1963 (18 days after the front page of the *Dallas Morning News* announced that JFK would be visiting Dallas in November), this same Ruth Paine placed a most fateful telephone call to Roy S. Truly, the superintendent of the Texas School Book Depository in downtown Dallas. As a direct result of that phone call, Lee Harvey Oswald began his employment at the Depository, which overlooked Dealey Plaza, where, some five weeks later, John Fitzgerald Kennedy was assassinated.

BOOK 3

CHAPTER

16

Covert Operations

As can be discerned from even our very brief glimpse of George de Mohrenschildt and his associates, American intelligence in the 50s and 60s might be described as being both 'passive' (receiving information) and 'active' (gun-running, etc.). But we have, to this point, seen just a tip of the iceberg of the 'active' side of the picture.

'Following the end of World War II, many nations in Eastern Europe and elsewhere fell under Communist influence or control. The defeat of the Axis powers was accompanied by rapid disintegration of the Western colonial empires. World War II had no sooner ended than a new struggle began. The Communist threat, emanating from what came to be called the "Sino-Soviet bloc", led to a policy of containment intended to prevent further encroachment into the "Free World".

'United States strategy for conducting the Cold War called for the establishment of interlocking treaty arrangements and military bases throughout the world. Concern over the expansion of an aggressive Communist monolith led the United States to fight two major wars in Asia. In addition, it was considered necessary to wage a relentless cold war against Communist expansion wherever it appeared in the "back alleys of the world". This called for a full range of covert activities in response to the operations of Communist clandestine services.

'The fear of Communist expansion was particularly acute in the United States when Fidel Castro emerged as Cuba's leader in the late 1950s. His takeover was seen as the first significant penetration by the Communists into the Western Hemisphere. United States leaders, including most Members of Congress, called for vigorous action to stem the Communist infection in this hemisphere. These policies rested on widespread support and encouragement.

'Throughout this period, the United States felt impelled to respond to threats which were, or seemed to be, skirmishes in a global Cold War against Communism. Castro's Cuba raised the specter of a Soviet outpost at America's doorstep. Events in the Dominican Republic appeared to offer an additional opportunity for the Russians and their allies. The Congo, freed from Belgian rule, occupied the strategic center of the African continent, and the prospect of Communist penetration there was viewed as a threat to American interests in emerging African nations. There was great concern that a Communist takeover in Indochina would have a "domino effect" throughout Asia. Even the election in 1970 of a Marxist president in Chile was seen by some as a threat similar to that of Castro's takeover in Cuba.[. . .]

'Covert action is activity which is meant to further the sponsoring nation's foreign policy objectives, and to be concealed in order to permit that nation to plausibly deny responsibility.[. . .]

'From 1955 to 1970, the basic authority for covert operations was a directive of the National Security Council, NSC5412/2. This directive instructed the CIA to counter, reduce and discredit "International Communism" throughout the world in a manner consistent with United States foreign and military policies. It also directed the CIA to undertal·e covert operations to achieve this end and defined covert operations as any covert activities related to propaganda, economic warfare, political action (including sabotage, demolition and assistance to resistance movements) and all activities compatible with the directive.[. . .]

'Beginning in 1955, the responsibility for authorizing CIA covert action operations lay with the Special Group, a subcommittee of the National Security Council composed of the President's Assistant for National Security Affairs, the Director of Central Intelligence, the Deputy Secretary of Defense and the Under Secretary of State for Political Affairs.'

A look at covert actions conducted in the Congo and the Dominican Republic should prove instructive for the material in following chapters.

'In the summer of 1960, there was great concern at the highest levels in the United States government about the role of Patrice Lumumba in the Congo. Lumumba, who served briefly as Premier of the newly independent nation, was viewed with alarm by United States policymakers because of what they perceived as his magnetic public appeal and his leanings toward the Soviet Union.

'Under the leadership of Lumumba and the new President, Joseph Kasavubu, the Congo declared its independence from Belgium on 30 June 1960. In the turbulent month that followed, Lumumba threatened to invite Soviet troops to hasten the withdrawal of Belgian armed forces. The United Nations Security Council requested Belgium's withdrawal and dispatched a neutral force to the Congo to preserve order. In late July, Lumumba visited Washington and received pledges of economic aid from Secretary of State Christian Herter. By the beginning of September, Soviet airplanes, trucks, and technicians were arriving in the province where Lumumba's support was strongest.[. . .]

'The evidence indicates that it is likely that President Eisenhower's expression of strong concern about Lumumba at a meeting of the National Security Council on 18 August 1960, was taken by Allen Dulles [Director of the CIA] as authority to assassinate Lumumba.[. . .]

'The week after the 18 August NSC meeting, a presidential advisor reminded the Special Group of the "necessity for very straightforward action" against Lumumba and prompted a decision not to rule out consideration of "any particular kind of activity which might contribute to getting rid of Lumumba". The following day, Dulles cabled a CIA Station Officer in Leopoldville, Republic of the Congo, that "in high quarters" the "removal" of Lumumba was "an urgent and prime objective". Shortly thereafter the CIA's clandestine service formulated a plot to assassinate Lumumba.[. . .]

'In the summer of 1960, DDP [Deputy Director for Plans] Richard Bissell asked the Chief of the Africa Division, Bronson Tweedy, to explore the feasibility of assassinating Patrice Lumumba. Bissell also asked a CIA scientist, Joseph Scheider, to make preparations to assassinate or incapacitate an unspecified "African leader". Scheider procured toxic biological materials in response to Bissell's request, and was then ordered by Tweedy to take these materials to the Station Officer in Leopoldville.[. . .]

'In mid-September, after losing a struggle for the leadership of the government to Kasavubu and Joseph Mobutu, Chief of Staff of the Congolese armed forces, Lumumba sought protection from the United Nations forces in Leopoldville.[. . .]

'The evidence indicates that the ouster of Lumumba did not alleviate the concern about him in the United States government. Rather, CIA and high Administration officials continued to view him as a threat. During this period, CIA officers in the Congo advised and aided Congolese contacts known to have an intent to assassinate Lumumba. The officers also urged the "permanent disposal" of Lumumba by some of these Congolese contacts. Moreover, the CIA opposed re-opening Parliament after the coup because of the likelihood that Parliament would return Lumumba to power.[. . .]

'In late September, Scheider delivered the lethal substances to the Station Officer in Leopoldville [Hedgman] and instructed him to assassinate Patrice Lumumba. The Station Officer testified that after requesting and receiving confirmation from CIA Head-quarters that he was to carry out Scheider's instruc-tions, he proceeded to take "exploratory steps" in furtherance of the assassination plot. . . .

'Scheider explained that the toxic material was to be injected into some substance that Lumumba would ingest: "it had to do with anything he could get to his mouth, whether it was food or a toothbrush, so that some of the material could get to his mouth".

'Hedgman said that the means of assassination was not restricted to use of toxic material provided by Scheider. He testified that he may have "suggested" shooting Lumumba to Scheider as an alternative to poisoning. Scheider said it was his "impression" that Tweedy and his Deputy empowered him to tell the Station Officer that he could pursue other means of assassination. Station Officer Hedgman testified that, although the selection of a mode of assassination was left to his judgement, there was a firm requirement that "if I implemented these instructions it had to be a way which could not be traced back either to an American or the United States government".[. . .]

'Scheider's mission to the Congo was preceded and followed by cables from Headquarters urging the "elimination" of Lumumba transmitted through an extraordinarily restricted "Eyes Only" channel – including two messages bearing the personal signature of Allen Dulles.'

The 'extraordinarily restricted' channel, known as

22 November 1963

The inscrutable face of Lee Harvey Oswald as he holds up his manacled hands shortly after his arrest.

(Copyright Ⓒ: AP Wirephoto)

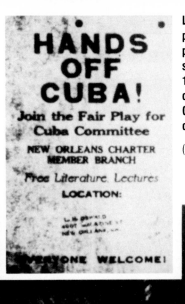

Lee Harvey Oswald, self-proclaimed Marxist, distributing pro-Castro propaganda on the streets of New Orleans in August 1963; but the address on the back of the handbills is that of anti-Castro activists with underworld connections.

(Warren Commission. Copyright Ⓒ: AP)

A youthful 19-year old Oswald photographed in his US Marine combat helmet while stationed in California.

(Copyright Ⓒ: AP Wirephoto)

The famous photograph of Oswald in his back yard with rifle, pistol and communist newspapers, captioned in Russian 'Hunter of Fascists, ha! ha! ha!' Incriminating evidence or elaborate fake? The shadows of the face fall in a different direction to those of the legs – the head is Oswald's but is the body?

24 November 1963

Jack Ruby steps forward, revolver levelled, as Lee Harvey Oswald is escorted through the Dallas city jail. A second later Ruby pumped a bullet into Oswald's stomach. He was never to stand trial – the shot was fatal. Ruby himself died in prison three years later, his own case unresolved.

(Copyright ©: *The Dallas Morning News*, 1963, via AP Wirephoto) the PROP channel, 'indicated extraordinary sensitivity and restricted circulation at CIA Headquarters to Dulles, Bissell, Tweedy, and Tweedy's Deputy. The PROP designator restricted circulation in the Congo to the Station Officer. Tweedy testified that the PROP channel was established and used exclusively for the assassination operation.[. . .]

'Throughout the fall of 1960, while Lumumba remained in UN protective custody, the CIA continued to view him as a serious political threat. One concern was that if Parliament were re-opened and the moderates failed to obtain a majority vote, the "pressures for Lumumba's return will be almost irresistible." Another concern at CIA Headquarters was that foreign powers would intervene in the Congo and bring Lumumba to power. Lumumba was also viewed by the CIA and the Administration as a stalking horse for "what appeared to be a Soviet effort to take over the Congo".'

On 15 October 1960, Bronson Tweedy dispatched a cable 'via the PROP channel for Hedgman's "Eyes Only", which prevented the message from being dispatched to anyone else, including the Ambassador'.

Amongst other things in this cable which dealt with the subject of the assassination of Lumumba, Tweedy requested 'the Station Officer's reaction to the prospect of sending a senior CIA case officer to the Congo on a "direct assignment to concentrate entirely this aspect".'

In his response two days later, Station Officer Hedgman concluded his cable 'with the following cryptic recommendation, reminiscent of his testimony that he may have "suggested" shooting Lumumba to Scheider as an alternative to poisoning: "If Case Officer sent, recommend HQS pouch soonest high powered foreign make rifle with telescopic scope and silencer. Hunting good here when lights right. However as hunting rifles now forbidden, would keep rifle in office pending opening of hunting season." Tweedy testified that the Station Officer's recommendation clearly referred to sending to the Congo via diplomatic pouch a weapon suited for assassinating Lumumba. The oblique suggestion of shooting Lumumba at the "opening of hunting season" could be interpreted as a plan to assassinate Lumumba as soon as he was seen outside the residence where he remained in UN protective custody. Tweedy interpreted the cable to mean that "an operational plan involving a rifle" had not yet been formulated by the Station Officer and that the "opening of hunting season" would depend upon approval of such a plan by CIA headquarters.[. . .]

'Michael Mulroney, a senior CIA officer in the Directorate for Plans, testified that in October 1960 he had been asked by Richard Bissell to go to the Congo to carry out the assassination of Lumumba.[. . .] At the time, Mulroney was the Deputy Chief of an extra-ordinarily secret unit within the Directorate of Plans.[. . .] Mulroney said that he refused to partici-pate in an assassination operation, but proceeded to the Congo to attempt to draw Lumumba away from the protective custody of the UN guard and place him in the hands of Congolese authorities.[. . .]

'According to Mulroney there was a "very, very high probability" that Lumumba would receive capital pun-ishment at the hands of the Congolese authorities. But he "had no compunction about bringing him out and then having him tried by a jury of his peers". Despite Mulroney's expressed aversion to assassination and his agreement to undertake a more general mission to "neutralize" Lumumba's influence, Bissell continued pressing him to consider an assassination opera-tion.[. . .]

'Shortly after Mulroney's arrival in the Congo, he was joined by QJ/WIN, a CIA agent with a criminal background. Late in 1960, WI/ROGUE, one of Hedgman's operatives, approached QJ/WIN with a proposition to join an "execution squad".[. . .]

'WI/ROGUE was an "essentially stateless" soldier of fortune, "a forger and former bank robber". The CIA sent him to the Congo after providing him with plastic surgery and a toupee so that Europeans traveling in the Congo would not recognize him.[. . .] CIA's Africa Division recommended WI/ROGUE as an agent in the following terms: "He is indeed aware of the precepts of right and wrong, but if he is given an assignment which may be morally wrong in the eyes of the world, but necessary because his case officer ordered him to carry it out, then it is right, and he will dutifully undertake appropriate action for its execution without pangs of conscience. In a word, he can rationalize all actions."'

A 14 November 1960 PROP cable from the Station Officer to Tweedy states that a CIA agent had learned that Lumumba's 'political followers in Stanleyville desire that he break out of his confinement and proceed to that city by car to engage in political activity . . . Decision on breakout will probably be made shortly. Station expects to be advised by [agent] of [what] decision was made . . . Station has several possible assets to use in event of breakout and studying several plans of action'.

Lumumba left UN custody on 27 November 1960. A cable the next day advised '[Station] working with [Congolese Government] to get roads blocked and troops alerted [block] possible escape route'. (CIA Cable, Leopoldville to Director, 28 November 1960.)

A CIA Cable on 29 November 1960 read, 'View change in location target, QJ/WIN anxious go Stanleyville and expressed desire execute plan by himself without using any apparat.'

The reply the following day from the Chief of the Africa Division to the Station Officer said 'Concur QJ/WIN go Stanleyville . . . We are prepared consider direct action by QJ/WIN but would like your reading on security factors. How close would this place [the United States] to the action?[. . .]

'Early in December, Mobutu's troops captured Lumumba while he was traveling toward his stronghold at Stanleyville and imprisoned him.[. . .]

'There is no doubt that the CIA and the Congolese government shared a concern in January 1961 that Lumumba might return to power, particularly since the Congolese army and police were threatening to mutiny if they were not given substantial pay raises.'

On 12 January 1961, 'Station Officer Hedgman reported that a mutiny "almost certainly would bring about [Lumumba] return power" and said he had advised the Congolese government of his opinion that the army garrison at Leopoldville "will mutiny within two or three days unless drastic action taken satisfy complaints".[. . .]

'The next day, Hedgman cabled Headquarters: "Station and Embassy believe present government may fall within few days. Result would almost certainly be chaos and return [Lumumba] to power." Hedgman advised that reopening the Congolese Parliament under United Nations supervision was unacceptable because: "The combination of [Lumumba's] powers as demagogue, his able use of goon squads and propaganda and spirit of defeat within [government] coalition which would increase rapidly under such conditions would almost certainly insure [Lumumba] victory in Parliament . . . Refusal take drastic steps at this time will lead to defeat of [United States] policy in Congo."[. . .]

'On 17 January, authorities in Leopoldville placed Lumumba and two of his leading supporters, Maurice Mpolo and Joseph Okito, aboard an airplane bound for Bakwanga. Apparently the aircraft was redirected in midflight to Elisabethville in Katanga Province "when it was learned that United Nations troops were at Bakwanga airport". On 13 February, the government of Katanga reported that Lumumba and his two companions escaped the previous day and died at the hands of hostile villagers.

'The United Nations Commission on Investigation was "not convinced by the version of the facts given by the provincial government of Katgana". The Commission concluded instead that Lumumba was killed on 17

January, almost immediately after his arrival in Katanga, probably with the knowledge of the central government and at the behest of the Katanga authorities: "The Commission wishes to put on record its view that President Kasavubu and his aides . . . should not escape responsibility for the death of Mr Lumumba, Mr Okito and Mr Mpolo. For Mr Kasavubu and his aides had handed over Mr Lumumba and his colleagues to the Katanga authorities knowing full well, in doing so, that they were throwing them into the hands of their bitterest political enemies."[. . .]

'[T]he Station Officer clearly had prior knowledge of the plan to transfer Lumumba to a state where it was probable that he would be killed. Other supporters of Lumumba who had been sent to Bakwanga earlier by Leopoldville authorities "were killed there in horrible circumstances, and the place was known as the 'slaughterhouse'."[. . .]

'Hedgman acknowledged that the CIA was in close contact with some Congolese officials who "quite clearly knew" that Lumumba was to be shipped to Katanga "because they were involved". But Hedgman said that these Congolese contacts "were not acting under CIA instructions if and when they did this".

'Rafael Trujillo came to power in the Dominican Republic in 1930. For most of his tenure, the United States Government supported him and he was regarded throughout much of the Caribbean and Latin America as a protégé of the United States. Trujillo's rule, always harsh and dictatorial, became more arbitrary during the 1950s. As a result, the United States' image was increasingly tarnished in the eyes of many Latin Americans.

'Increasing American awareness of Trujillo's brutality and fear that it would lead to a Castro-type revolution caused United States officials to consider various plans to hasten his abdication or downfall.

'As early as February 1960, the Eisenhower Administration gave high level consideration to a program of covert aid to Dominican dissidents.[. . .] During the spring of 1960, the US Ambassador to the Dominican Republic, Joseph Farland, made initial contact with . . . a group of dissidents regarded as moderate, pro-United States and desirous of establishing a democratic form of government.[. . .] 'During the course of a cocktail party in the Dominican Republic, a leading dissident made a specific request to Ambassador Farland for a limited number of rifles with telescopic sights. The Ambassador promised to pass on the request. He apparently did so after returning to Washington.[. . .]

'Prior to his final departure from the Dominican Republic in May 1960, the Ambassador introduced his Deputy-Chief-of-Mission, Henry Dearborn, to the dissident leaders, indicating that Dearborn could be trusted.

'Then on 16 June 1960, CIA Headquarters cabled a request that Dearborn become the "communications link" between the dissidents and CIA. The cable stated that Dearborn's role had the unofficial approval of Assistant Secretary of State for Inter-American Affairs, Roy R. Rubottom. Dearborn agreed. He requested, however, that the CIA confirm the arrangement with the dissidents as being that the United States would "clandestinely" assist the opposition to "develop effective force to accomplish Trujillo overthrow", but would not "undertake any overt action itself against Trujillo government while it is in full control of Dominican Republic". CIA Headquarters confirmed Dearborn's understanding of the arrangement.[. . .]

'Events occurring during the summer of 1960 further intensified hemispheric opposition to the Trujillo regime. In June, agents of Trujillo tried to assassinate Venezuelan President Betancourt. As a result, the OAS (Organization of American States) censured the Trujillo government. At the same time, in August 1960 the United States interrupted diplomatic relations with the Dominican Republic and imposed economic sanctions. With the interruption of diplomatic relations, the United States closed its Embassy. Most American personnel, including the CIA Chief of Station, left the Dominican Republic. With the departure of the CIA Chief of Station, Dearborn became *de facto* CIA Chief of Station and was recognized as such by both CIA and the State Department. Although in January 1961 a new CIA Chief of Station came to the Dominican Republic, Dearborn continued to serve as a link to the dissidents.

'Dearborn came to believe that no effort to overthrow the Trujillo government could be successful unless it involved Trujillo's assassination. He communicated this opinion to both the State Department and the CIA.[. . .]

'On 19 January 1961, the last day of the Eisenhower Administration, Consul General Dearborn was advised that approval had been given for supplying arms and other material to the Dominican dissidents.[. . .]

'In a 15 March 1961 cable, a Station officer reported that Dearborn had asked for three .38 caliber pistols for issue to several dissidents.[. . .] [A] 7 June 1961 CIA memorandum, unsigned and with no attribution as to source, states that two of the three pistols were passed by a Station officer to a United States citizen who was in direct contact with the action element of the dissident group.[. . .]

'In a 26 March 1961 cable to CIA Headquarters, the Station asked for permission to pass to the dissidents three 30 caliber M1 carbines. The guns had been left behind in the Consulate by Navy personnel after the United States interrupted formal diplomatic relations in August 1960 . . . On 31 March 1961, CIA Headquarters cabled approval of the request to pass the carbines. The carbines were passed to the action group contact on 7 April 1961. Eventually, they found their way into the hands of one of the assassins, Antonio de la Maza.[. . .]

'On 7 April 1961, a Pouch Restriction Waiver

Request and Certification was submitted seeking permission to pouch "four M3 machine guns and 240 rounds of ammunition on a priority basis for issuance to a small action group to be used for self protection" . . . The Waiver Request was approved by Richard Bissell, as DDP, on 10 April 1961 . . . The machine guns were pouched to the Dominican Republic and were received by the Station on 19 April 1961.[. . .]

'By 17 April 1961, the Bay of Pigs invasion had failed. As a result, there developed a general realization that precipitous action should be avoided in the Dominican Republic until Washington was able to give further consideration to the consequences of a Trujillo overthrow and the power vacuum which would be created. A cable from Headquarters to the Station, on 17 April 1961, advised that it was most important that the machine guns not be passed without additional Headquarters approval.[. . .]

'Dearborn recalls receiving instructions that an effort be made to turn off the assassination attempt and testified that efforts to carry out the instructions were unsuccessful. In effect, the dissidents informed him that this was their affair and it could not be turned off to suit the convenience of the United States government.

'On 30 April, 1961, Dearborn advised Headquarters that the dissidents had reported to him the assassination attempt was going to take place during the first week of May. The action group was reported to have in its possession three carbines, four to six 12-gauge shotguns and other small arms. Although they reportedly still wanted the machine guns, Dearborn advised Headquarters that the group was going to go ahead with what they had, whether the United States wanted them to or not.'

State Department memoranda dated 15 May stressed that it was 'highly desirable for the United States to be identified with and to support the elements seeking to overthrow Trujillo [and] recommended that Consul General inform the dissidents that if they succeed "at their own initiative and on their own responsibility in forming an acceptable provisional government they can be assured that any reasonable request for assistance from the US will be promptly and favorably answered".'[. . .]

'Late in the evening of 30 May 1961, Trujillo was ambushed and assassinated near San Cristobal, Dominican Republic. The assassination closely paralleled the plan disclosed by the action group to American representatives in the Dominican Republic and passed on to officials in Washington at both the CIA and the State Department. The assassination was conducted by members of the action group, to whom the American carbines had been passed, and such sketchy information as is available indicates that one or more of the carbines was in the possession of the assassination group when Trujillo was killed. The evidence indicates, however, that the actual assassination was accomplished by handguns and shotguns.'

BOOK 3

CHAPTER 17

Strange Bedfellows

As noted previously, '[T]he fear of Communist expansion was particularly acute in the United States when Fidel Castro emerged as Cuba's leader in the late 1950s. His takeover was seen as the first significant penetration by the Communists into the Western Hemisphere. United States leaders, including most Members of Congress, called for vigorous action to stem the Communist infection in this hemisphere. These policies rested on widespread popular support and encouragement. Throughout this period, the United States felt impelled to respond to threats which were, or seemed to be, skirmishes in a global Cold War against Communism. Castro's Cuba raised the specter of a Soviet outpost at America's doorstep . . .'

After discussing other countries, the Senate Select Committee went on to a lengthy study of the Cuban situation.

'Efforts against Castro did not begin with assassination attempts. From March through August 1960, during the last year of the Eisenhower Administration, the CIA considered plans to undermine Castro's charismatic appeal by sabotaging his speeches.

'According to the 1967 Report of the CIA's Inspector General, an official in the Technical Services Division (TSD) recalled discussing a scheme to spray Castro's broadcasting studio with a chemical which produced effects similar to LSD, but the scheme was rejected because the chemical was unreliable. During this period, TSD impregnated a box of cigars with a chemical which produced temporary disorientation, hoping to induce Castro to smoke one of the cigars before delivering a speech.

'The Inspector General also reported a plan to destroy Castro's image as "The Beard" by dusting his shoes with thallium salts, a strong depilatory that would cause his beard to fall out. The depilatory was to be administered during a trip outside Cuba, when it was anticipated Castro would leave his shoes outside the door of his hotel room to be shined. TSD procured the chemical and tested it on animals, but apparently abandoned the scheme because Castro cancelled his trip.[. . .]

'A notation in the records of the Operations Division, CIA's Office of Medical Services, indicates that on 16 August 1960 an official was given a box of Castro's favorite cigars with instructions to treat them with lethal poison. The cigars were contaminated with a botulinum toxin so potent that a person would die after putting one in his mouth. The official reported that the cigars were ready on 7 October 1960; TSD notes indicate that they were delivered to an unidentified person on 13 February 1961. The record does not disclose whether an attempt was made to pass the cigars to Castro.[. . .]

'In August 1960, the CIA took steps to enlist members of the criminal underworld with gambling syndicate contacts to aid in assassinating Castro.[. . .]

'The earliest concrete evidence of the operation is a conversation between DDP Bissell and Colonel Sheffield Edwards, Director of the Office of Security. Edwards recalled that Bissell asked him to locate someone to assassinate Castro. Bissell confirmed that he requested Edwards to find someone to assassinate Castro and believed that Edwards raised the idea of contacting members of a gambling syndicate operating in Cuba. Edwards assigned the mission to the Chief of the Operational Support Division of the Office of Security.[. . .]

'Edwards and the Support Chief decided to rely on Robert A. Maheu to recruit someone "tough enough" to handle the job. Maheu was an ex-FBI agent who had entered into a career as a private investigator in 1954. A former FBI associate of Maheu's was employed in the CIA's Office of Security and had arranged for the CIA to use Maheu in several sensitive covert operations in which "he didn't want to have an Agency person or a government person get caught". Maheu was initially paid a monthly retainer by the CIA of $500, but it was terminated after his detective agency became more lucrative. The Operational Support Chief had served as Maheu's case officer since the Agency first began using Maheu's services, and by 1960 they had become close personal friends.

'Sometime in late August or early September 1960, the Support Chief approached Maheu about the proposed operation.' It was decided that Maheu 'would contact John Rosselli, an underworld figure with possible gambling contacts in Las Vegas, to determine if he would participate in a plan to "dispose" of Castro . . . Maheu had known Rosselli since the late 1950s. [. . .]

'At first Maheu was reluctant to become involved in the operation because it might interfere with his relationship with his new client, Howard Hughes. He finally agreed to participate because he felt that he owed the Agency a commitment. . . . The Support Chief testified that Maheu was told to offer money, probably $150,000, for Castro's assassination.

'According to Rosselli, he and Maheu met at the Brown Derby Restaurant in Beverly Hills in early September 1960. Rosselli testified that Maheu told him that "high government officials" needed his cooperation in getting rid of Castro, and that he asked him to help recruit Cubans to do the job.[. . .]

'Maheu and Rosselli both testified that Rosselli insisted on meeting with a representative of the Government. A meeting was arranged for Maheu and Rosselli with the Support Chief at the Plaza Hotel in New York.[. . .]

'It was arranged that Rosselli would go to Florida and recruit Cubans for the operation.[. . .] During the week of 24 September 1960 the Support Chief, Maheu, and Rosselli met in Miami to work out the details of the operation.[. . .] After Rosselli and Maheu had been in Miami for a short time, and certainly prior to 18 October, Rosselli introduced Maheu to individuals on whom Rosselli intended to rely: "Sam Gold", who would serve as a "back-up man", or "key" man, and "Joe", whom "Gold" said would serve as a courier to Cuba and make arrangements there.[. . .]

'The Support Chief testified that he learned the true identities of his associates one morning when Maheu called and asked him to examine the "Parade" supplement to the *Miami Times*. An article on the Attorney General's ten most-wanted criminals list revealed that "Sam Gold" was Momo Salvatore Giancana, a Chicago-based gangster, and "Joe" was Santos Trafficante, the Cosa Nostra chieftain in Cuba.'

Momo Salvatore ('Sam') Giancana was not exactly a candidate for monkhood. In addition to his more obvious disqualifications, Sam would have had serious problems with the vow of silence. In an 18 October 1960 memo to Richard Bissell, J. Edgar Hoover reported that Giancana had recently told several friends that Fidel Castro was to be done away with shortly by a girl dropping a pill into his drink. The Committee related that 'The identity of this "girl" referred to by Giancana has not been conclusively ascertained, but it is reasonable to assume that Trafficante was in a position to recruit a mistress of Castro because of his numerous contacts in the Cuban gambling and prostitution circles.'

Nor was silence the only monk's vow with which Giancana would have had difficulty. He had a great fondness for the women. One of his girl friends in Las Vegas became the center of a bizarre event – bizarre if only because it was such an eerie precursor of the Watergate foul-up.

'In late October 1960, Maheu arranged for a Florida investigator, Edward DuBois, to place an electronic "bug" in a room in Las Vegas. Dubois' employee, Arthur J. Balletti, flew to Las Vegas and installed a tap on the phone. The Support Chief characterized the ensuing events as a "Keystone Comedy act". On 31 October 1960, Balletti, believing that the apartment would be vacant for the afternoon, left the wiretap equipment unattended. A maid discovered the equipment and notified the local sheriff, who arrested Balletti and brought him to the jail. Balletti called Maheu in Miami, tying "Maheu into this thing up to his ear". Balletti's bail was paid by Rosselli.[. . .]

'The Support Chief testified that during the early stages of negotiations with the gambling syndicate, Maheu informed him that a girl-friend of Giancana was having an affair with the target of the tap. Giancana wanted Maheu to bug that person's room; otherwise, Giancana threatened to fly to Las Vegas himself. Maheu was concerned that Giancana's departure would disrupt the negotiations, and secured the Support Chief's permission for a bug to insure Giancana's presence and cooperation.[. . .]

'Rosselli testified that Maheu had given him two explanations for the tap on different occasions: first, that Giancana was concerned that his girl-friend was having an affair; and, second, that he had arranged the tap to determine whether Giancana had told his girl friend about the assassination plot, and whether she was spreading the story.'

During the investigation of this affair, Colonel Edwards mislead the FBI, informing the Bureau that 'the CIA would object to Maheu's prosecution because it might reveal sensitive information relating to the abortive Bay of Pigs invasion'. Subsequently, 'Herbert J. Miller, Assistant Attorney General, Criminal Division, advised the Attorney General that the "national interest" would preclude any prosecutions based upon the tap. Following a briefing of the Attorney General by the CIA, a decision was made not to prosecute.'

Another of Giancana's girl-friends, Judith Campbell Exner, reportedly was introduced to John F. Kennedy by Frank Sinatra, and a long-term 'relationship' between her and JFK bloomed until it was brought to a sudden and unceremonious end when J. Edgar Hoover intervened.

The Committee circumspectly reported this affair as follows: 'Evidence before the Committee indicates that a close friend of President Kennedy had frequent contacts with the President from the end of 1960 through mid-1962; FBI reports and testimony indicate that the President's friend was also a close friend of John Rosselli and Sam Giancana and saw them often during this same period . . . White House telephone logs show 70 instances of phone contact between the White House and the President's friend, whose testimony confirms frequent phone contact with the President himself . . . On 27 February 1962, Hoover sent identical copies of a memorandum to the Attorney General and Kenneth O'Donnell, Special Assistant to the President. The memorandum stated that information developed in connection with a concentrated FBI investigation of John Rosselli revealed that Rosselli had been in contact with the President's friend. The memorandum also reported that the individual was maintaining an association with Sam Giancana, described as "a prominent Chicago underworld figure". Hoover's memorandum also stated that a review of the telephone toll calls from the President's friend's residence revealed calls to the White House.[. . .]

'The association of the President's friend with the "hoodlums" and that person's connection with the President was again brought to Hoover's attention in a memorandum preparing him for a meeting with the President planned for 22 March 1962 . . . On 22 March, Hoover had a private luncheon with President Kennedy. There is no record of what transpired at that luncheon. According to the White House logs, the last telephone contact between the White House and the President's friend occurred a few hours after the luncheon.'

The Senate Select Committee was curious about the claim made by the Support Chief that he first learned the identities of Sam Gold and Joe because of an article in the "Parade" supplement of the *Miami Times*. We learn from the 1978 House Committee Report that in 1975 the Senate Committee had 'conducted a search of supplements to all Miami newspapers for the requisite time period and could not locate any such article. The Committee consequently searched "Parade" magazine for the fall of 1960, all of 1961, and all of 1962, the years that spanned the entire operation. The Committee found that on 21 January 1962, "Parade" published an article entitled "The Untold Story: Our Government's Crackdown on Organized Crime", written by Jack Anderson, which contained a listing of the top 10 hoodlums in the country as well as several photographs of mobsters, including Santos Trafficante. The article focused on the efforts of Attorney General Robert F. Kennedy's campaign against organized crime and mentioned both Giancana and Trafficante. Although this "Parade" article appears to correspond with the Support Chief's and Maheu's descriptions, it is over 1 year past the beginning months of the operation. Indeed, it occurred 9 months after the completion of Phase I of the plots'.

The House Committee goes on to comment: 'It

appears the Support Chief and Maheu are not telling the truth in an attempt to look for an ex-*post facto* reason for continuing the operation after the introduction of two of the top organized crime figures in the United States. Implicit in their contention is that while the CIA wished to solicit criminal sources to assassinate Castro, it would not knowingly have recruited any figures from the top echelon of organized crime.[. . .]

'[T]his CIA plot to assassinate Castro was necessarily a highly volatile and secret operation. Once Roselli introduced additional contacts into the scene, it is not logical that the CIA would have neglected to verify the identities of such principals. On the contrary, it is more believable that the CIA ascertained the true identities of "Sam Gold" and "Joe" at an early stage and progressed consciously forward in the operation, confident that these two persons, in the words attributed to Colonel Sheffield Edwards, were individuals "tough enough" to handle the job.'

'After meeting several times in Miami and deciding upon poison pills as the method of assassination, the IG report [Inspector General] states that Trafficante made the arrangements for the assassination of Castro with one of his contacts inside Cuba on one of the trips he allegedly made to Havana, Cuba. This contact was a Cuban official who held a position close to Castro. ¡

'The IG report then stated that Rosselli passed the pills to Trafficante. Rosselli subsequently told the Support Chief that the pills were delivered to the Cuban official in Cuba. The Cuban official apparently retained the pills for a few weeks and then returned them since he was no longer in a position to fulfill any plan. The Cuban official was no longer in a position to kill Castro because he had lost his Cuban post.

'With the Cuban official unable to perform, the syndicate looked elsewhere. Rosselli next told the Support Chief, sometime during early 1961, that Trafficante knew a man prominent in the Cuban exile movement who could accomplish the job. After receiving approval, Trafficante approached this person about assassinating Castro and reported that he was receptive. The IG report stated that the Support Chief again distributed pills that eventually reached the Cuban exile leader.'

The Senate Report states: 'The Cuban claimed to have a contact inside a restaurant frequented by Castro.[. . .] The attempt met with failure. According to the Inspector General's Report, Edwards believed the scheme failed because Castro stopped visiting the restaurant where the "asset" was employed.[. . .]

'The Inspector General's Report divides the gambling syndicate operation into Phase I, terminating with the Bay of Pigs, and Phase II, continuing with the transfer of the operation to William Harvey in late 1961. The distinction between a clearly demarcated Phase I and Phase II may be an artificial one, as there is considerable evidence that the operation was continuous, perhaps lying dormant for the period immediately following the Bay of Pigs.

'In early 1961, Harvey was assigned the responsibility for establishing a general capability within the CIA for disabling foreign leaders, including assassination as a "last resort". The capability was called Executive Action and was later included under the cryptonym ZR/RIFLE.[. . .]

'Harvey's notes reflect that Bissell asked him to take over the gambling syndicate operation from Edwards and that they discussed the "application of ZR/RIFLE program to Cuba" on 16 November 1961.'

The House Report informs us that, 'The Support Chief then introduced Harvey to Rosselli. During this phase, the CIA decided against using Giancana or Trafficante; instead, a person referred to as "Maceo" entered the plot as the person who would help provide Castro contacts. In addition, the plots still utilized the services of the Cuban exile leader.[. . .]

'In June 1962 Rosselli reported to Harvey that the

Cuban exile leader dispatched a three-man team to Cuba with the general assignment of recruiting others to kill Castro and, if the opportunity arose, to kill him themselves, maybe through the use of pills. In September 1962, Rosselli reported to Harvey in Miami that the "medicine" was reported in place, that the three-man team was safe, and that the Cuban exile leader was prepared to dispatch another three-man team to infiltrate Castro's bodyguard. In December 1962, Rosselli and Harvey agreed that not much seemed to be occurring and by February 1963, Harvey terminated the plots.'

The Senate Report states that 'Two plans to assassinate Castro were explored by Task Force W, the CIA section then concerned with covert Cuban operations, in early 1963. Desmond Fitzgerald, Chief of the Task Force, asked his assistant to determine whether an exotic seashell, rigged to explode, could be deposited in an area where Castro commonly went skin diving. The idea was explored by the Technical Services Division and discarded as impractical.

'A second plan involved having James Donovan (who was negotiating with Castro for the release of prisoners taken during the Bay of Pigs operation) present Castro with a contaminated diving suit.[. . .] The Technical Services Division bought a diving suit, dusted the inside with a fungus that would produce a chronic skin disease (Madura foot), and contaminated the breathing apparatus with a tubercule bacillus. The Inspector General's Report states that the plan was abandoned because Donovan gave Castro a different diving suit on his own initiative. Helms testified that the diving suit never left the laboratory [and characterized the plan as "cockeyed"].'

In the fall of 1963, another operation against Castro began. Since early 1961, the CIA had had an important asset inside Cuba in the person of a highly-placed Cuban official who was referred to by the cryptonym AM/LASH.

'As a high-ranking leader who enjoyed the confidence of Fidel Castro, AM/LASH could keep the CIA informed of the internal workings of the regime. It was also believed that he might play a part in fomenting a coup within Cuba.

'From the first contact with AM/LASH until the latter part of 1963, it was uncertain whether he would defect or remain in Cuba. His initial requests to the CIA and FBI for aid in defecting were rebuffed.[. . .]

'At a meeting in the fall of 1963, AM/LASH stated that he would remain in Cuba if he "could do something really significant for the creation of a new Cuba" and expressed a desire to plan the "execution" of Fidel Castro.' Desmond Fitzgerald, Chief of the Special Affairs Staff (formerly called Task Force W) 'met AM/LASH in late fall 1963 and promised him that the United States would support a coup against Castro. When later interviewed for the Inspector General's Report, Fitzgerald recalled that AM/LASH repeatedly requested an assassination weapon, particularly a "high-powered rifle with telescopic sights that could be used to kill Castro from a distance". Fitzgerald [originator of the exploding seashell brainstorm] stated that he told AM/LASH that the United States would have "no part of an attempt on Castro's life".' However, a contemporaneous memorandum by the case officer involved states 'C/SAS [Fitzgerald] approved telling AM/LASH he would be given a cache inside Cuba. Cache could, if he requested it, include . . . high-powered rifles with scopes.[. . .] AM/LASH was told on 22 November 1963 that the cache would be dropped in Cuba.

'Another device offered to AM/LASH was a ballpoint pen rigged with a hypodermic needle. The needle was designed to be so fine that the victim would not notice its insertion.[. . .] Helms confirmed that the pen was manufactured "to take care of a request from him that he have some device for getting rid of Castro, for killing him, murdering him, whatever the case may be".

[. . .] On 22 November, 1963, Fitzgerald and the case officer met with AM/LASH and offered him the poison pen, recommending that he use Blackleaf-40, a deadly poison which is commercially available. The Inspector General's Report noted that "it is likely that at the very moment President Kennedy was shot, a CIA officer was meeting with a Cuban agent . . . and giving him an assassination device for use against Castro." [. . .]

'CIA cables indicate that one cache of arms for AM/LASH was delivered in Cuba in March 1964 and another in June.[. . .] Documents in the AM/LASH file establish that in early 1965, the CIA put AM/LASH in contact with B-1, the leader of an anti-Castro group.[. . .] In June 1965, CIA terminated all contact with AM/LASH and his associates for reasons related to security.'

BOOK 3

CHAPTER

18

Castro Retaliation?

In March 1967, President Lyndon Johnson learned of allegations which had recently been asserted by a Washington lawyer named Edward Morgan, and that the FBI had refused to investigate the charges.

Morgan was saying that one of his clients had told him that the United States had attempted to assassinate Fidel Castro in the early 1960s, and Castro had decided to retaliate.

President Johnson instructed 'that the FBI interview [the lawyer] concerning any knowledge he might have regarding the assassination of President Kennedy'. On 21 March 1967, two agents of the Washington Field Office sent FBI Headquarters a memorandum of their interview with Morgan.

The Senate Select Committee summarized the memo as follows:

'(1) The lawyer had information pertaining to the assassination, but that it was necessary for him in his capacity as an attorney to invoke the attorney-client privilege since the information in his possession was derived as a result of that relationship.

'(2) His clients, who were on the fringe of the

underworld, were neither directly nor indirectly involved in the death of President Kennedy, but they faced possible prosecution in a crime not related to the assassination and through participation in such crime they learned of information pertaining to the President's assassination.

'(3) His clients were called upon by a governmental agency to assist in a project which was said to have the highest governmental approval. The project had as its purpose the assassination of Fidel Castro. Elaborate plans were made; including the infiltration of the Cuban government and the placing of informants within key posts in Cuba.

'(4) The project almost reached fruition when Castro became aware of it; by pressuring captured subjects he was able to learn the full details of the plot against him and decided "if that was the way President Kennedy wanted it, he too could engage in the same tactics".

'(5) Castro thereafter employed teams of individuals who were dispatched to the United States for the purpose of assassinating President Kennedy. The lawyer stated that his clients obtained this information "from 'feedback' furnished by sources close to Castro", who had been initially placed there to carry out the original project.

'(6) His clients were aware of the identity of some of the individuals who came to the United States for this purpose and he understood that two such individuals were now in the State of New Jersey.

'(7) One client, upon hearing the statement that Lee Harvey Oswald was the sole assassin of President Kennedy "laughs with tears in his eyes and shakes his head in apparent disagreement".

'(8) The lawyer stated if he were free of the attorney-client privilege, the information that he would be able to supply would not directly identify the alleged conspirators to kill President Kennedy. However, because of the project to kill Fidel Castro, those participating in the project, whom he represents, developed through feedback information that would identify Fidel Castro's counter-assassins in this country who could very well be considered suspects in such a conspiracy.

'The transmittal slip accompanying this memorandum noted, "No further investigation is being conducted by the Washington Field Office unless it is advised to the contrary by the Bureau."[. . .]

'Both agents testified that they were "surprised" during the interview when the lawyer recounted United States assassination efforts targeted at Fidel Castro. These agents stated that they could not evaluate the lawyer's allegations or question him in detail on them, since they had not been briefed on the CIA assassination efforts.'

The House Select Committee observed, 'Had the interviewing agents known of the CIA-underworld plots against Castro, they would have been aware that the lawyer had clients who had been active in the assassination plots . . . Neither the Field agents who interviewed the lawyer nor the Headquarters supervisory agents assigned to the assassination case could provide any explanation for the Bureau's failure to conduct any follow-up investigation. When they were informed of the details of CIA assassination efforts against Castro, each of these agents stated that the allegations and specific leads provided should have been investigated to their logical conclusions.'

The concept of a Castro retaliation theory has been discounted on the following rationalizations:

(1) That Castro has denied it.

(2) That it would not make sense for Castro to do it.

(3) That Morgan's client was manipulating the facts.

(4) That Castro didn't know about the US plots against him.

The first two items are easily dealt with by asking the

questions: Why would anyone believe Castro's denial, and what grounds are there for assuming that Castro would have been so logical?

The third item refers to the fact that one of Morgan's clients was John Rosselli, who was at the time trying to avoid deportation. There is no doubt that given such a source, one must take any information with a large grain of salt. However, the fact that the source is a Rosselli does not necessarily mean the information is untrue. Indeed, if the government really believed that such a source necessarily made information untrue, they would have to drop a very large percentage of their criminal prosecutions since they are based on 'turning' someone. The fact is that much of law enforcement is premised on the reality that only when a Rosselli is being threatened by some penalty to be imposed upon himself, will he divulge information as to others. Moreover, the first part of the information Morgan was supplying is now known to be true.

Consideration of the balance of Morgan's information leads us to item four, the proposition that Castro could not have known about US plots against him and so would have had no reason to retaliate.

It will be recalled that an intricate part of the CIA-Mafia plot against Castro involved Salvatore Trafficante's role as a courier. The IG Report states that, 'At that time the gambling casinos were still operating in Cuba, and Trafficante was making regular trips between Miami and Havana on syndicate business.'

The House Select Committee observed, 'If Trafficante was actually traveling between Miami and Havana, the implications are interesting. He was either willing to risk being detained again or had acquired assurance from the Cuban Government regarding his safety. In any event, the presence of Trafficante during the fall of 1960 in Cuba raises the possibility of a more cooperative relationship between himself and the Cuban Government than believed previously. Such a relationship during the period when Trafficante was scheming to assassinate Castro invites the theory that Trafficante was possibly informing the Cuban Government of activities in the Miami area in general and of the plots in particular. In return for such information, Trafficante could have been promised lost gambling operations as well as support and a Cuban sanctuary for the smuggling of contraband into the United States.'

Trafficante was not the only potential source for Castro to learn of the US plots against his life. Joseph Langosch, the Chief of Counter-Intelligence for the CIA's Special Affairs Staff in 1963 (the component responsible for CIA operations against the Government of Cuba and the Cuban Intelligence Services) told the House Select Committee that 'The AM/LASH operation prior to the assassination of President Kennedy was characterized by the special affairs staff, Desmond FitzGerald and other senior CIA officers as an assassination operation initiated and sponsored by the CIA . . . [A]s of 1962 it was highly possible that the Cuban Intelligence Services were aware of AM/LASH and his association with the CIA.'

Any question that Castro knew of the US plots against his life would seem to be resolved by this quote from the Report of the House Select Committee regarding 'an interview that Premier Castro held on 7 September 1963 with Associated Press Reporter Daniel Harker. In that interview, Castro warned against the United States "aiding terrorist plans to eliminate Cuban leaders". He stated, according to Harker, that US leaders would be in danger if they promoted any attempt to eliminate the leaders of Cuba.'

None of this proves that President Kennedy was assassinated by Castro in retaliation for US assassination plots against him. However, possible Castro retaliation plots are not the only Cuban aspect to our story.

In fact, in one fashion or another, Cuba lies at the very center of this web.

BOOK 3

CHAPTER

19

Anti-Castro Cubans

The House Select Committee, after an exhaustive analysis of the whole Cuban situation, stated that, '[T]he Committee ascertained that as a consequence of the efforts, the failure and the eventual unwillingness of the Kennedy administration to liberate Cuba from Castro, [anti-Castro activists and organizations] acquired the means, motive and opportunity to assassinate the President.'

In addition to its Report, the House published a special study on this subject in which it observed: 'If it can be said to have a beginning, the anti-Castro Cuban exile movement was seeded in the early-morning hours of New Year's Day 1959 when a DC-4 lifted from the fog-shrouded Camp Columbia airfield in Havana. Aboard the plane was Fulgencio Batista, the military dictator of Cuba for the previous 6 years. Batista was fleeing the country, his regime long beset by forces from within and without, now crumbling under pressure from rebel forces sweeping down from the mountains. When dawn came, the bells tolled in Havana and, 600 miles away, Fidel Castro Ruz began his triumphal march to the capital. For seven days

Castro and his 26th of July Movement rebels moved down Cuba's Central Highway while thousands cheered and threw flowers in their path. Castro finally arrived in Havana on 8 January and characteristically gave a speech. Clad in his green fatigue uniform while three white doves, which someone had dramatically released, circled above him, Castro boldly proclaimed: "There is no longer an enemy!"

'That was not true, of course, and he knew it. A hard core of Batistianos had fled the country early, many long before their leader, and were already concocting counter-revolutionary plots from their refuges in the United States, the Dominican Republic and elsewhere.

'And it was not very long after Castro took power that a sense of betrayal began to grow among those who had once been his strongest supporters. As each day went by it became more apparent that Castro's revolution was, as one chronicler noted, "leading inexorably toward an institutionalized dictatorship in which individuals were contemptuously shorn of their rights and dissenters were met with charges of treasonable conduct, counter-revolutionary activity or worse". Then, too, there was a large number of public executions. Within 2 weeks of his reign, Castro shot 150 ex-Batista officials. Within 3 months, there were at least 506 executions.

'The disillusionment for many Cubans deepened when it became obvious that the form of Castro's rule was turning toward Communism and that Castro's attitude toward the United States was engendering a hostile relationship. The publishing of Castro's Agrarian Reform Law in May 1959, was a significant sign. It was far more radical than had been expected and was obviously designed to strip both Cuban and American-owned sugar firms of their immensely valuable cane lands. A few weeks later the chief of Castro's air force, Major Pedro Diaz-Lanz, resigned, charging "there was Communist influence in the armed forces and Government". Then, when Castro's own hand-picked president, Manuel Urrutia, announced at a press conference that he rejected the support of the Communists and said,. "I believe that any real Cuban revolutionary should reject it openly", Castro immediately forced him to resign and accused him of actions "bordering on treason".

'And so, after the broken pledges of free elections and a free press, the mass trials and executions, the assumption of unlimited power and the bellicose threats against the United States, it slowly became apparent to many Cubans that Fidel Castro was not the political savior they had expected.

'Then, on 19 October 1959, there occurred an incident which precipitated the formation of the first organized anti-Castro opposition within Cuba. Major Huber Matos, one of Castro's highest ranking officers and considered by most Cubans to be one of the key heroes of the revolution, resigned from the Army in protest against the increasing favoritism shown to known Communists. The next day Matos was arrested, charged with treason, subsequently tried and sentenced to 20 years in prison. Shortly afterward, Castro himself called a secret meeting of the National Agrarian Reform Institute managers at which he outlined a plan to communize Cuba within three years. There the suspicions of Dr Manuel Artime, the manager in Oriente Province, were confirmed. "I realized," Artime later said, "that I was a democratic infiltrator in a Communist government".

'Artime returned to Oriente and began organizing students and peasants to fight against Castro and Communism. By early November each province in Cuba had an element of Artime's new underground movement. It was called the Movimiento de Recuperación Revolucionaria (MRR). It was the first anti-Castro action group originating from within Castro's own ranks.

'By the summer of 1960, it had become obvious both within and without Cuba that the foundation for an eventual confrontation between Castro and anti-Castro forces had been laid. The Eisenhower administration had canceled the Cuban sugar quota. Soviet first deputy chairman Anastas Mikoyan had visited Havana and Raul Castro had gone to Moscow. Ernesto "Che" Guevara had proclaimed publicly that the revolution was on the road set by Marx, and Allen Dulles of the Central Intelligence Agency had said in a speech that Communism had perverted Castro's revolution. By then, Castro had seized more than $700 million in US property within Cuba.

'On 17 March 1960, President Eisenhower authorized the CIA to organize, train and equip Cuban refugees as a guerilla force to overthrow Castro. Soon it became common knowledge within Cuba that a liberation army was being formed and that a political structure in exile had been created. As the flight from Cuba increased in size and fervor, the exile community in the United States grew in spirit and confidence.[. . .]

'By April 1961, the more than 100,000 Cubans who had fled Castro's revolution lived in anticipation of its overthrow. They had been buoyed in that hope by public pronouncements of support from the US Government. In his State of the Union Address, President Kennedy had spoken of "the Communist base established 90 miles from the United States", and said that "Communist domination in this hemisphere can never be negotiated". In addition, the Cuban exiles had been organized, directed and almost totally funded by agencies of the US Government, principally the CIA.

'From an historical perspective, in light of its later radical change, the attitude of the Cuban exiles toward the US Government prior to the Bay of Pigs is especially significant. Author Haynes Johnson who in writing a history of the invasion collaborated with the top Cuban leaders, including brigade civilian chief Manuel Artime, described that attitude in detail: "From the beginning, the Cuban counter-revolutionists viewed their new American friends with blind trust. Artime was no exception. He, and later virtually all of the Cubans involved, believed so much in the Americans – or wanted so desperately to believe – that they never questioned what was happening or expressed doubts about the plans. Looking back on it, they agree now that their naiveté was partly genuine and partly reluctance to turn down any offer of help in liberating their country. In fact, they had little choice; there was no other place to turn. Some, of course, were driven by other motives: political power and personal ambition were involved. Even more important was the traditional Cuban attitude toward America and Americans. To Cubans the United States was more than the colossus of the north, for the two countries were bound closely by attitudes, by history, by geography and by economics. The United States was great and powerful, the master not only of the hemisphere but perhaps of the world, and it was Cuba's friend. One really didn't question such a belief. It was a fact; everyone knew it. And the mysterious, anonymous, ubiquitous American agents who dealt with the Cubans managed to strengthen that belief."

'This "blind trust" by the Cuban exiles in the US Government prior to the Bay of Pigs was specifically noted by the military commander of the 2506 Brigade, Jose (Pepe) Perez San Roman: "Most of the Cubans were there", he said, "because they knew the whole operation was going to be conducted by the Americans, not by me or anyone else. They did not trust me or anyone else. They just trusted the Americans. So they were going to fight because the United States was backing them."

'The débâcle at the Bay of Pigs was not only military tragedy for the anti-Castro Cuban exiles but also a painful shattering of their confidence in the US Government. The exile leaders claimed the failure of the invasion was a result of the lack of promised air support, and for that they directly blamed President Kennedy. Particularly galling to them was Kennedy's public declaration to Soviet Premier Khrushchev at the height of the invasion, when the Brigade was being slaughtered in the swamps of Bahia de Cochinos: "I repeat now that the United States intends no armed intervention in Cuba."

'Even those exile leaders who were willing to rationalize the extent of Kennedy's responsibility were dissuaded when Kennedy himself admitted the blame. Cuban Revolutionary Council leader Manuel Antonio de Varona, in his executive session testimony before the Committee, told of the President gathering the Council members together at the White House when it became clear that the invasion was a disaster. Varona recalled: "We were not charging Mr Kennedy with anything; we just wanted to clarify. We knew that he didn't have any direct knowledge of the problem, and we knew he was not in charge of the military effects directly. Nevertheless, President Kennedy, to finish the talks, told us he was the one – the only one responsible."

'A few days after that meeting, the White House issued a public statement declaring that President Kennedy assumed "sole responsibility" for the US role in the action against Cuba.

'The acceptance of responsibility did not cut the bitter disappointment the Cuban exiles felt toward the US Government and President Kennedy. Much later, captured and imprisoned by Castro, Brigade Commander San Roman revealed the depth of his reaction at the failure of the invasion: "I hated the United States," he said, "and I felt that I had been betrayed. Every day it became worse and then I was getting madder and madder and I wanted to get a rifle and come and fight against the US."

'Prominent Cuban attorney Mario Lazo wrote a book caustically titled *Dagger in the Heart*. Lazo wrote: "The Bay of Pigs defeat was wholly self-inflicted in Washington. Kennedy told the truth when he publicly accepted responsibility . . . The heroism of the beleaguered Cuban Brigade had been rewarded by betrayal, defeat, death for many of them, long and cruel imprisonment for the rest. The Cuban people and the Latin American nations, bound to Cuba by thousands of subtle ties of race and culture, were left with feelings of astonishment and disillusionment, and in many cases despair. They had always admired the United States as strong, rich, generous – but where was its sense of honor and the capacity of its leaders? The mistake of the Cuban fighters for liberation was that they thought too highly of the United States. They believed to the end that it would not let them down. But it did."

'President Kennedy was well aware of the bitter legacy left him by the Bay of Pigs débâcle. It is not now possible to document the changes in Kennedy's personal attitude brought about by the military defeat, but the firming of US policy toward Cuba and the massive infusion of US aid to clandestine anti-Castro operations in the wake of the Bay of Pigs was editorially characterized by Taylor Branch and George Crile in *Harper's Magazine* as "the Kennedy vendetta".

'What can be documented is the pattern of US policy between the period of the Bay of Pigs failure in April 1961 and the Cuban missile crisis in October 1962. That pattern, replete with both overt and covert maneuvers, had a significant effect on the reshaping of Cuban exile attitudes and, when it was abruptly reversed, could have provided the motivation for involvement in the assassination of President Kennedy.

'In retrospect, the period between the Bay of Pigs and the Cuban missile crisis can be considered the high-water mark of anti-Castro activity, almost every manifestation of the US policy providing a reassurance of support of the Cuban cause. As a matter of fact, only a few days after the Bay of Pigs invasion, President Kennedy delivered a particularly hard-line address before the American Society of Newspaper Editors on the implications of Communism in Cuba. "Cuba must not be abandoned to the Communists", he declared. In appealing for support from Latin America, he indicated that the United States would expect more from the nations of the hemisphere with regard to Cuba and asserted that the United States would not allow the doctrine of non-intervention to hinder its policy. Said Kennedy, "Our restraint is not inexhaustible", and spoke of Cuba in the context of the "new and deeper struggle".

'When Castro, in a May Day speech, declared Cuba to be a socialist nation, the State Department retorted that Cuba was a full-fledged member of the Communist bloc.

'Another US response was the establishment of the Alliance for Progress, after years of relatively little attention to Latin America's economic and social needs. President Kennedy gave the Alliance concept a memorable launching in a speech in March 1961 when he called for vigorous promotion of social and economic development in Latin America through democratic means and, at the same time, pledged substantial financial and political support.

'While the campaign to broaden its Cuban policy base was being pursued, the United States was proceeding on another course. In one of the first unilateral efforts to isolate Cuba from its allies, the United States in September 1961 announced it would stop assistance to any country that assisted Cuba. In December, Kennedy extended the denial of Cuba's sugar quota through the first half of 1962.

'Meanwhile, the secret policy aimed at removing Castro through assassination continued as FBI chief J. Edgar Hoover informed Attorney General Robert Kennedy in May that the CIA had used the Mafia in "clandestine efforts" against Castro. In that month, poison pills to be used in a plot to kill Castro were passed to a Cuban exile in Miami by a Mafia figure. In November 1961, Operation Mongoose, designed to enlist 2,000 Cuban exiles and dissidents inside Cuba to overthrow Castro, was initiated.

'Although the bitter after-taste of the Bay of Pigs invasion lingered in the Cuban exile community, those who remained active in the fight against Castro came to realize that these subsequent actions of the Kennedy administration were manifestations of its determination to reverse the defeat. What Kennedy had euphemistically termed "a new and deeper struggle" became, in actuality, a secret war.

'The nerve center of the United States' "new and deeper struggle" against Castro was established in the heartland of exile activity, Miami. There, on a secluded, heavily wooded 1,571-acre tract that was part of the University of Miami's south campus, the CIA set up a front operation, an electromics firm called Zenith Technological Services. Its code name was JM/WAVE and it soon became the largest CIA installation anywhere in the world outside of its headquarters in Langley, Virginia.

'The JM/WAVE station had, at the height of its activities in 1962, a staff of more than 300 Americans, mostly case officers. Each case officer employed from 4 to 10 Cuban "principal agents" who, in turn, would each be responsible for between 10 and 30 regular agents.

'In addition, the CIA set up 54 front corporations – boat shops, real estate firms, detective agencies, travel companies, gun shops – to provide ostensible employment for the case officers and agents operating outside of JM/WAVE headquarters. It also maintained hundreds of pieces of real estate, from small apartments to palatial homes, as "safe houses" in which to hold secret meetings. As a result of its JM/WAVE operation, the CIA became one of Florida's largest employers.

'It was the JM/WAVE station that monitored, more or less controlled, and in most cases funded the anti-Castro groups. It was responsible for the great upsurge in anti-Castro activity and the lifted spirits of the Cuban exiles as American arms and weapons flowed freely through the training camps and guerilla bases spotted around south Florida. Anti-Castro raiding parties that left from small secret islands in the Florida Keys were given the "green light" by agents of the JM/WAVE station. The result of it all was that there grew in the Cuban exile community a renewed confidence in the US Government's sincerity and loyalty to its cause.

'Then came the Cuban missile crisis. The more fervent Cuban exiles were initially elated by the possibility that the crisis might provoke a final showdown with Castro.

'For several months there had been increasing pressure on President Kennedy to take strong measures against the build-up of the Soviet presence in Cuba, which was becoming daily more blatant. In a report issued at the end of March 1962, the State Department said that Cuba had received from the Soviet Union $100 million in military aid for the training of Cuban pilots in Czechoslovakia and that the Soviet Union also had provided from 50 to 75 Mig fighters as well as tons of modern weapons for Cuba's ground forces. Fortifying the Cuban exiles' hope for action was the fact that the increasing amounts of Soviet weapons moving into Cuba became the dominant issue in the news in the succeeding months, leading to congressional calls for action and a series of hard-line responses from President Kennedy. In September, Kennedy declared that the United States would use "whatever means may be necessary" to prevent Cuba from exporting "its aggressive purposes by force or threat of force" against "any part of the Western Hemisphere".

'The fervent hope of the Cuban exiles – that the Cuban missile crisis would ultimately result in the United States smashing the Castro regime – was shattered by the manner in which President Kennedy resolved the crisis. Cuba itself was relegated to a minor role as tough negotiations took place between the United States and Soviet Union, specifically through communication between President Kennedy and Premier Khrushchev.

'The crisis ended when President Kennedy announced that all IL-28 bombers were being withdrawn by the Soviets and progress was being made on the withdrawal of offensive missiles and other weapons from Cuba.

'In return, Kennedy gave the Soviets and the Cubans a "no invasion" pledge.

'If Kennedy's actions at the Bay of Pigs first raised doubts in the minds of the Cuban exiles about the President's sincerity and determination to bring about the fall of Castro, his handling of the missile crisis confirmed those doubts. Kennedy's agreement with Khrushchev was termed "a violation" of the pledge he had made 3 days after the Bay of Pigs invasion that the United States would never abandon Cuba to Communism. Wrote one prominent exile: "For the friendly Cuban people, allies of the United States, and for hundreds of thousands of exiles eager to stake their lives to liberate their native land, it was a soul-shattering blow."

'The bitterness of the anti-Castro exiles was exacerbated by the actions the US Government took to implement the President's "no invasion" pledge Suddenly there was a crackdown on the very training camps and guerilla bases which had been originally established and funded by the United States, and the exile raids which once had the Government's "green light" were now promptly disavowed and condemned.

'On 31 March 1963, a group of anti-Castro raiders were arrested by British police at a training site in the Bahamas. The US State Department admitted it had given the British the information about the existence of the camp. That same night another exile raiding boat was seized in Miami Harbor. On 3 April, the Soviet Union charged that the United States "encourages and bears full responsibility" for two recent attacks on Soviet ships in Cuban ports by anti-Castro exile commandos. The United States responded that it was "taking every step necessary to insure that such attacks are not launched, manned or equipped from US territory". On 5 April, the Coast Guard announced it was throwing more planes, ships, and men into its efforts to police the straits of Florida against anti-Castro raiders. As a result of the crackdown, Cuban exile sources declared that their movement to rid their homeland of Communism had been dealt "a crippling blow" and that they had lost a vital supply link with anti-Castro fighters inside Cuba.

'There were numerous other indications of the US crackdown on anti-Castro activity following the missile crisis. The Customs Service raided what had long been a secret training camp in the Florida Keys and arrested the anti-Castro force training there. The FBI seized a major cache of explosives at an anti-Castro camp in Louisiana. Just weeks later, the US Coast Guard in cooperation with the British Navy captured another group of Cuban exiles in the Bahamas. In September, the Federal Aviation Administration issued "strong warnings" to six American civilian pilots who had been flying raids over Cuba. Shortly afterward, the Secret Service arrested a prominent exile leader for conspiring to counterfeit Cuban currency destined for rebel forces inside Cuba. In October, the Coast Guard seized 4 exile ships and arrested 22 exile raiders who claimed they were moving their operations out of the United States.

'The feeling of betrayal by the Cuban exiles was given reinforcement by prominent sympathizers outside their community, as well as by Kennedy's political opponents. Captain Eddie Rickenbacker, chairman of the Committee for the Monroe Doctrine, asserted: "The Kennedy administration has committed the final betrayal of Cuban hopes for freedom by its order to block the activities of exiled Cuban freedom fighters to liberate their nation from Communism." Senator Barry Goldwater accused Kennedy of "doing everything in his power" to keep the flag of Cuban exiles "from ever flying over Cuba again". Richard Nixon urged the end of what he called the "quarantine" of Cuban exiles.

'Of course, the most strident reactions came from within the anti-Castro community itself. Following the US Government's notification that it would discontinue its subsidy to the Cuban Revolutionary Council, its president, Jose Miro Cardona, announced his resignation from the council in protest against US policy. The Cuban exile leader accused President Kennedy of "breaking promises and agreements" to support another invasion of Cuba. Miro Cardona said the change in American policy reflected the fact that Kennedy had become "the victim of a master play by the Russians". [. . .]

'Against the pattern of US crackdown on Cuban exile activity during this period, however, emerges a countergrain of incidents that may have some bearing on an examination of the Kennedy assassination. These incidents involve some extremely significant Cuban exile raids and anti-Castro operations which took place, despite the crackdown, between the time of the missile crisis and the assassination of the President. [. . .]

'In retrospect, this much is clear. With or without US Government support and whether or not in blatant defiance of Kennedy administration policy, there were a number of anti-Castro action groups which were determined to continue – and, in fact, did continue – their operations. The resignation of Miro Cardona actually split the Cuban Revolutionary Council down the middle and precipitated a bitter dispute among the exile factions. The more moderate contended that without US support there was little hope of ousting Castro and that the exiles should concentrate their efforts in mounting political pressure to reverse Washington's shift in policy. Other exile groups announced their determination to continue the war against Castro and, if necessary, to violently resist the curtailment of their para-military activities in the Kennedy administration. In New Orleans, for instance, Carlos Bringuier, the local leader of the Cuban Student Directorate (DRE) who, coincidentally, would later have a contact with Lee Harvey Oswald, proclaimed, in the wake of the Miro Cardona resignation, that his group "would continue efforts to liberate Cuba despite action by the United States to stop raids originating from US soil".

'The seeds of defiance of the Kennedy administration may have been planted with the exiles even prior to the Bay of Pigs invasion. In his history of the invasion, Haynes Johnson revealed that shortly before the invasion, "Frank Bender", the CIA director of the invasion preparations, assembled the exile leaders together at the CIA's Guatemala training camp: "It was now early in April and Artime was in the camp as the civilian representative of the Revolutionary Council. Frank called Pepe (San Roman) and (Erneido) Oliva again. This time he had startling information. There were forces in the administration trying to block the invasion, and Frank might be ordered to stop it. If he received such an order, he said, he would secretly inform Pepe and Oliva. Pepe remembers Frank's next words this way: 'If this happens you come here and make some kind of show, as if you were putting us, the advisers, in prison, and you go ahead with the program as we have talked about it, and we will give you the whole plan, even if we are your prisoners.' . . . Frank then laughed and said: 'In the end we will win.'"

'That, then, is the context in which the Committee approached the question of whether or not the John F. Kennedy assassination was a conspiracy involving anti-Castro Cuban exiles. It also considered the testimony of the CIA's chief of its Miami JM/WAVE station in 1963, who noted, "'assassination' was part of the ambience of that time".'

As the quote attributed to 'Frank Bender' makes clear, there was rather less than total respect and admiration for President Kennedy by at least some CIA personnel. This was, it should be noted, not a one-way street.

Although Kennedy accepted 'sole responsibility' for

the Bay of Pigs débâcle, privately he blamed the CIA. Use here of the word 'privately' should not be misunderstood to mean 'secretly'; it really is used to distinguish Kennedy's true feelings from his 'official' statements. He didn't make much of a secret about his disdain for the CIA, which was such that, as the House Report relates, he vowed to 'splinter the agency into a thousand pieces'.

The net result of all of this was that John Kennedy wound up with two sets of enemies who shared mutual interests and the capacity for violence.

BOOK 3

CHAPTER

20

Kennedy Had Enemies

Elements of the CIA, and anti-Castro Cubans, were not John Kennedy's only bitter enemies.

'In an era when the United States was confronted with intractable, often dangerous, international and domestic issues, the Kennedy administration was inevitably surrounded by controversy as it made policies to deal with the problems it faced. Although a popular President, John F. Kennedy was reviled by some, an enmity inextricably related to his policies. [. . .]

'Kennedy appointed Blacks to high administration posts and to Federal judgeships. He gave Attorney General Robert F. Kennedy his sanction for vigorous enforcement of civil rights laws to extend voting rights, end segregation and fight racial discrimination. [. . .]

'Violence erupted soon after Kennedy took office. In May 1961, the Congress of Racial Equality staged a series of freedom rides in Alabama in an effort to integrate buses and terminals. One bus was burned by a mob in Anniston, Alabama. An angry segregationist crowd attacked demonstrators in Montgomery, Alabama, and several persons were injured. Attorney

General Kennedy ordered several hundred US marshals to Montgomery to protect the demonstrators. National Guardsmen with fixed bayonets scattered a mob that tried to overwhelm the marshals, who were protecting a mass meeting at a Black church where civil rights leader Martin Luther King, jun., was speaking. [. . .]

'Trouble exploded again in 1962 when James Meredith, a 29-year-old Black Air Force veteran, gained admission to the all-white University of Mississippi. Meredith had been refused admission, despite Federal court orders requiring that he be enrolled. The Kennedy administration supported an effort to force compliance by the State, but Governor Ross Barnett was equally determined to defy the orders. In his fourth attempt to enroll at the university, Meredith arrived in Oxford on 30 September, escorted by 300 US marshals. He was met by a mob of 2,500 students and segregationist extremists who howled, "Two four one three, we hate Kennedy . . ." A bloody night-long riot that left two dead and scores injured was quelled only after Federal troops had been dispatched by President Kennedy. [. . .]

'Blacks continued demonstrations for equal rights in the spring of 1963. In April and May, Dr King led an attack on what he called "the most segregated city in the United States", Birmingham, Alabama. Demonstrators were met by police dogs, electric cattle prods and fire hoses. [. . .]

'In June 1963, Alabama Governor George Wallace, in defiance of a Federal court order, stood on the steps of the University of Alabama to prevent the admission of two Black students. Wallace bowed, however, to National Guard troops that had been federalized by the President . . . In the same month, Medgar Evers, the NAACP field secretary for Mississippi, was shot to death in front of his home in Jackson, Mississippi. [. . .]

'On 28 August 1963, an inter-racial group of more than 200,000 persons joined "The March for Jobs and

Freedom" in Washington, DC, to urge the Congress to pass the comprehensive civil rights legislation the Kennedy administration envisioned. Violence shattered the hopeful mood in the wake of the Washington march when a bomb exploded on 17 September at the Sixteenth Street Baptist Church in Birmingham, Alabama during a Sunday School session. Four young Black girls were killed and 23 other persons were injured. [. . .]

'In October, *Newsweek* magazine reported that the civil rights issue alone had cost Kennedy 3.5 million votes, adding that no Democrat in the White House had ever been so disliked in the South. In Georgia, the marquee of a movie theatre showing *PT109* read "See how the Japs almost got Kennedy". [. . .]

'As the policies of the Kennedy administration broke new ground, political extremists in the United States seemed increasingly willing to resort to violence to achieve their goals. In an address at the University of Washington in Seattle on 16 November 1961, President Kennedy discussed the age of extremism: two groups of frustrated citizens, one urging surrender and the other urging war. He said: "It is a curious fact that each of these extreme opposites resembles the other. Each believes that we have only two choices: appeasement or war, suicide or surrender, humiliation or holocaust, to be either Red or dead."

'The radical right condemned Kennedy for his "big Government" policies, as well as his concern with social welfare and civil rights progress. The ultra-conservative John Birch Society, Christian Anti-Communist Crusade led by Fred C. Schwarz, and the Christian Crusade led by Revd Billy James Hargis attracted an anti-Kennedy following. The right wing was incensed by Kennedy's transfer of General Edwin A. Walker from his command in West Germany to Hawaii for distributing right-wing literature to his troops. The paramilitary Minutemen condemned the administration as "soft on Communism" and adopted guerilla warfare tactics to prepare for the fight against the Communist foe. At the other extreme, the left labeled Kennedy a reactionary disappointment, a tool of the "power elite".'

There was, however, another domestic issue which presented President Kennedy with, perhaps, his foremost enemy – an enemy all the more dangerous to him since it had contacts with, and could mobilize and utilize segments of, his other enemies.

BOOK 3

CHAPTER

21

Enemy No. 1, The Mob

The House Committee, in its special volume on organized crime, relates that, 'Up to the 1960s the . . . groups of organized crime were in an enviable position. They had an organization that few believed existed and about which little was known. Its leaders – and hence the organization itself – were protected by low-level members who actually performed the criminal acts, many of which Federal and other agencies considered to be beyond their purview or legislative mandate. At best, organized crime was assigned a low priority at State and local levels of law enforcement, and even this was easily nullified by corruption and politics. At the Federal level, even where there was concern, effective action was hampered by inadequate enabling legislation. [. . .]

'The only major national investigation to be conducted during the period from prohibition until the late 1950s was that of the Senate Select Committee to Investigate Organized Crime in Interstate Commerce, chaired by Senator Estes Kefauver. The Committee held hearings in major cities across the country. It built up a substantial body of knowledge that indicated that there was a national and highly successful syndicate known as the Mafia, involved in a wide range of criminal activities throughout the United States and abroad. Violence was key to its success, as was corruption, and it was completely ruthless. As a result of the Committee's findings, Congress passed some gambling legislation, similar investigations were precipitated at the State and local levels, and in 1954, the Federal Government took further action by setting up the Organized Crime and Racketeering Section in the Department of Justice. Its main function was to coordinate the effort against organized crime, but it found little cooperation from other agencies.

'It was in 1957 that organized crime once again came into national attention. On 14 November, a significant meeting took place outside the village of Appalachian, New York. The aftermath was perhaps not what the participants had anticipated, for not only was the cloak of secrecy partially pulled aside, but the event ultimately led to the greatest campaign to date against organized crime.

'On that day, Sergeant Edgar Crosswell of the New York State Police noted that a large number of people were converging on the estate of Joseph Barbera, sen., many from far away. Crosswell had long been interested in Barbera, at the time the distributor for a major soda bottling company. Barbera had come from northern Pennsylvania, where he had a long police record that included two arrests for homicide (he was not convicted of either).

'Because the meeting was on private property, no direct police action could be taken. Crosswell himself watched the entrance from nearby. A tradesman from the village, while making a delivery, noticed Crosswell and alerted those at the meeting.

'Many of Barbera's guests elected to depart. Some did so by car and were detained, once on public roads, for the purpose of identification. Others who fled onto adjoining posted acreage were picked up for possible trespass. Most of those who remained on Barbera's estate could not be identified.

'In all, 63 people were detained and identified. Local hotel records, auto rental contracts and one report of a motor vehicle accident provided investigators with the names of still others. The evidence showed that they had come from New England, New York, New Jersey, Pennsylvania, Florida, Missouri, Texas, Colorado, Ohio, Illinois, and northern and southern California. They included many of the leading organized crime figures, such as Santos Trafficante, Vito Genovese, Carmine Galante, John Ormento and Sam Giancana . . . The evidence supported a conclusion that the gathering was to have been a national meeting of . . . criminals and their associates. [. . .]

'Because a number of attendees at the Appalachian meeting were directly or indirectly involved in union affairs, some were called before the Senate Select Committee on Improper Activities in the Labor or Management Fields, chaired by Senator John L. McClellan. These hearings became known as the McClellan Committee hearings. Senator John F. Kennedy was a member of this Committee; his brother, Robert F. Kennedy, was its chief counsel. [. . .]

'By 1960, the FBI had accumulated substantial knowledge about . . . organized criminal groups . . . Nevertheless, the FBI did not make organized crime a top priority until the Kennedy administration arrived in Washington . . . With the advent of [the Kennedy] administration, organized crime investigations were assigned a high priority . . . As a first step, Robert Kennedy dramatically expanded the number of attorneys in the Organized Crime and Racketeering Section of the Criminal Division of the Justice Department and made clear to the FBI that organized crime was to be a high priority. The category within which these investigations were carried at Justice was shown in FBI files to be AR, or anti-racketeering. He also put together a list of 40 organized crime figures who were to be targeted for investigation. This was soon followed by a second list of 40. The Attorney General quickly requested new legislation to improve the Department's ability to attack organized crime. [. . .]

'The scope and success of this campaign by the Kennedy administration can be easily seen in the following . . . Between 1960 (prior to the Kennedy administration) and 1963, there was:

(1) A 250 percent increase in the number of attorneys – from 17 to 60.

(2) More than a 900 percent increase in days in the field – from 660 to 6,172

(3) A 1,250 percent increase in days in grand jury – from 100 to 1,353.

(4) A 1,700 percent increase in days in court – from 61 to 1,081.

From 1961 to 1963, there was:

(1) A 500 percent increase in defendants indicted – from 121 to 615.

(2) A 400 percent increase in defendants convicted – from 73 to 288. [. . .]

'As the year 1963 progressed, there were many signs that the constant pressure was taking its toll.'

As the House Committee stated in its final report: 'The zeal of the Kennedy brothers signified the roughest period for organized crime in Department of Justice history. Historian Arthur Schlesinger, jun., wrote in *Robert Kennedy and His Times* that, as a result of the Attorney General's pressure, the national Government took on organized crime as it had never done before". Schlesinger observed: "In New York, Robert Morgenthau, the Federal Attorney, successfully prosecuted one syndicate leader after another. The Patriarca gang in Rhode Island and the De Cavalcante gang in New Jersey were smashed. Convictions of racketeers by the Organized Crime Section [together with] the Tax Division steadily increased – 96 in 1961, 101 in 1962, 373 in 1963. So long as John Kennedy sat in the White House, giving his Attorney General absolute backing, the underworld knew that the heat was on."

'The Attorney General focused on targets he had become acquainted with as counsel for the Rackets Committee. He was particularly concerned about the alliance of the top labor leaders and racketeers as personified by Teamster President James R. Hoffa. Schlesinger wrote that "the pursuit of Hoffa was an aspect of the war against organized crime". He added: "The relations between the Teamsters and the syndicate continued to grow. The FBI electronic microphone, planted from 1961 to 1964 in the office of Anthony Giacalone, a Detroit hood, revealed Hoffa's deep if wary involvement with the local mob. For national purposes a meeting place was the Rancho La Costa Country Club near San Clemente, California, built with $27 million in loans from the Teamsters' pension fund; its proprietor, Morris B. Dalitz, had emerged from the Detroit [sic. Cleveland] underworld to become a Las Vegas and Havana gambling figure. Here the Teamsters and the mob golfed and drank together. Here they no doubt reflected that, as long as John Kennedy was President, Robert Kennedy would be unassailable."'

Schlesinger may well be right that Jimmy Hoffa came to realize that the key was John, not Robert, since John could always replace Robert; but if John were gone, Robert was out of office. However, the House Select Committee found that 'Hoffa and at least one of his Teamster lieutenants, Edward Partin, apparently did, in fact, discuss the planning of an assassination conspiracy against President Kennedy's brother, Attorney General Robert F. Kennedy, in July or August of 1962 . . . In an interview with the Committee, Partin reaffirmed the account of Hoffa's discussion of a possible assassination plan, and he stated that Hoffa had believed that having the Attorney General murdered would be the most effective way of ending the Federal Government's intense investigation of the Teamsters and organized crime. Partin further told the Committee that he suspected that Hoffa may have approached him about the assassination proposal because Hoffa believed him to be close to various figures in Carlos Marcello's syndicate organization. Partin, a Baton Rouge Teamsters official with a criminal record, was then a leading Teamsters Union official in Louisiana . . . While the Committee was aware of the apparent absence of any finalized method or plan during the course of Hoffa's discussion about assassinating Attorney General Kennedy, he did discuss the possible use of a lone gunman equipped with a rifle with a telescopic sight, the advisability of having the assassination committed somewhere in the South, as well as the potential desirability of having Robert Kennedy shot while riding in a convertible . . . Edward Partin told the Committee that Hoffa believed that by having Kennedy shot as he rode in a convertible, the origin of the fatal shot would be obscured . . . The context of Hoffa's discussion with Partin about an assassination conspiracy further seemed to have been predicated upon the recruitment of an assassin without any identifiable connection to the Teamster organization or Hoffa himself.'

The special organized crime volume of the House Committee Report informs us that by 1963, 'Santos Trafficante's gambling operations in Florida were in trouble. [. . .] Sam Giancana in Chicago was also feeling the pressure. Giancana's concern could be readily understood. For some time he had been the subject of intense coverage by the FBI. By the spring of 1963, it had become "bumper-to-bumper", almost 24 hours per day – while driving, on the golf course, in restaurants, wherever he was . . . As a consequence, Giancana was staying away from his home base in Chicago to a significant degree, and it was creating problems. [. . .]

'Later in July 1963, on two weekends, Sam Giancana and Phyllis McGuire, the singer, were together at the Cal-Neva Lodge on Lake Tahoe, Nevada. One of these weekends Frank Sinatra, who owned 50 percent of the Lodge (as well as having an interest in the Sands in Las Vegas) was with them. On 2 August 1963 Giancana and McGuire were also guests at Frank Sinatra's Palm Springs, California, home, having flown there on Sinatra's plane. These and other similar facts appeared in the Chicago newspapers and other media and resulted in action by the Nevada Gaming Commission, which had listed Giancana as a person not to be allowed in any premises licenced for gambling. Sinatra refused to deny his close relationship with Giancana and decided to sell his interests rather than run the risk of a suspended licence. Later that month, the FBI learned of rumbling in the higher echelons of organized crime in Chicago over Giancana's absenteeism and bad publicity.'

Other La Cosa Nostra leaders were also experiencing difficulties, but few more than Carlos Marcello. 'The FBI determined in the 1960s that because of Marcello's position as head of the New Orleans Mafia family (the oldest in the United States, having first entered the country in the 1880s), the Louisiana organized crime leader had been endowed with special powers and privileges not accorded to any other La Cosa Nostra leaders. As the leader of "the first family" of the Mafia in America, according to FBI information, Marcello has been the recipient of the extraordinary privilege of conducting syndicate operations without having to seek the approval of the national commission.'

In a special section dealing exclusively with Carlos Marcello, the House Committe relates, 'The exact place of Marcello's birth on 6 February 1910 has long been in doubt, and at one point was a central question in a lengthy deportation proceeding. Nevertheless, it is generally believed that Marcello was born in Tunis, North Africa, with the name Calogero Minacore.

'Marcello's first contact with the law came on 29 November 1929, when he was arrested at the age of 19 by New Orleans police as an accessory before and after the robbery of a local bank. The charges were subsequently dismissed. Less than 6 months later, on 13 May 1930, he was convicted of assault and robbery and was sentenced to the State penitentiary for 9 to 14 years. He served less than 5 . . . In 1935, after receiving a pardon by the Governor of Louisiana, Marcello's early underworld career continued, with charges being filed against him for a second assault and robbery, violation of Federal Internal Revenue laws, assault with intent to kill a New Orleans police officer, and yet another assault and robbery. Marcello was not prosecuted on the various charges. In 1938, as part of what Federal agents described as "the biggest marihuana ring in New Orleans history", Marcello was arrested and charged with the sale of more than 23 pounds of illegal substance. Despite receiving another lengthy prison sentence and a $76,830 fine, Marcello served less than 10 months and arranged to settle his fine for $400. Other charges were brought against Marcello over the next several years, stemming from such alleged offenses as narcotics sale, a high speed automobile chase, and assaulting an investigative reporter; these were never prosecuted, and the records have since disappeared.

'During the 1940s, Marcello became associated with New York Mafia leader Frank Costello in the operation of a slot machine network. Costello was then regarded by some authorities as one of the most influential leaders of organized crime in the United States and was commonly referred to in the newspapers as the Mafia's "boss of all bosses" or "prime minister of the underworld". Marcello's association with Costello in various Louisiana gambling activities had come about following a reported agreement between Costello and Senator Huey Long that allowed for the introduction of slot machines into New Orleans.

'Marcello was also involved in Louisiana gambling through his family-owned Jefferson Music Company, which came to dominate the slot machine, pinball and juke box trade in the New Orleans area. By the late

1940s, in an alliance with Joseph Poretta, Marcello had taken control of the largest racing wire service in New Orleans, the Southern News Service and Publishing Co., which served Louisiana's prosperous gambling network. Marcello and other associates also gained control of the two best-known gambling casinos in the New Orleans area, the Beverly Club and New Southport Club; the Beverly Club brought Marcello into partnership with the syndicate financier, Meyer Lansky.

'By the late 1950s, the Nola Printing Co. of New Orleans, a gambling wire service controlled by the Marcello interests, was serving bookmakers and relay centers throughout the State of Louisiana, as well as areas as diverse as Chicago, Houston, Miami, Hot Springs, Indianapolis and Detroit and cities in Alabama and Mississippi.

'In a statement prepared for the House Judiciary Committee in 1970, [Aaron M. Kohn, the managing director of the Metropolitan Crime Commission of New Orleans and a former FBI agent] outlined the continuing expansion of Marcello's holdings during the 1940s and 1950s: "Marcello and his growing association developed their capital or bankroll through extensive gambling, including casinos, slot machines, pinball, handbooks, layoff, football pools, dice card games, roulette and bingo; also narcotics, prostitution, extortion, clipjoint operations, B-drinking, marketing stolen goods, robberies, burglaries, and thefts. Their criminal enterprise required, and had, corrupt collusion of public officials at every critical level including police, sheriffs, justices of the peace, prosecutors, mayors, governors, judges, councilmen, licencing authorities, State legislators, and at least one Member of Congress."

'When Marcello appeared as a witness before the Kefauver Committee on 25 January 1951, he invoked the fifth amendment and refused to respond to questioning on his organized crime activities. Subsequently convicted of contempt of Congress for refusing to respond to the directions of the chair, Marcello was later successful in having his conviction overturned. In its final report, the Kefauver Committee concluded that Marcello's domination of organized crime in Louisiana had come about in large part due to the "personal enrichment of sheriffs, marshals, and other law enforcement officials" who received payoffs for "their failure to enforce gambling laws and other statutes relating to vice". The Kefauver report further noted that, "In every line of inquiry, the Committee found . . . the trail of Carlos Marcello."

'The Kefauver report also raised the question of why Marcello, who "has never become a citizen", "had not been deported".

'In early 1953, partly as a result of the national attention he received from the Kefauver Committee investigation, Marcello finally became the subject of deportation proceedings. [. . .]

'Carlos Marcello was called to testify before the McClellan Committee on 24 March 1959, during the Committee's extended investigation of labor racketeering and organized crime. Serving as chief counsel to the Committee was Robert F. Kennedy; his brother, Senator John F. Kennedy, was a member of the Committee. In response to Committee questioning, Marcello again invoked the fifth amendment in refusing to answer any questions relating to his background, activities, and associates.

'At the conclusion of Marcello's appearance before the Committee, Senator Sam Ervin of North Carolina requested of the Chair permission to ask the New Orleans underworld leader one final question: "I would like to know how you managed to stay in the United States for 5 years, 9 months and 24 days after you were found ordered deported as an undesirable person." Marcello's response to the question – "I wouldn't know" – provoked Ervin to state that "the American people's patience ought to run out on this" and that "those who have no claim to any right to remain in America, who come here and prey like leeches upon law-abiding people ought to be removed from this country". Senator Karl Mundt joined in Ervin's denunciation, urging prompt action by the Attorney General, and Senator Carl Curtis further remarked to Marcello that, "I think you ought to pack up your bags and voluntarily depart." [. . .]

'Carlos Marcello and his syndicate became a primary target of investigation by the Department of Justice during the Kennedy administration. Attorney General Robert F. Kennedy viewed him as one of the most powerful and threatening Mafia leaders in the Nation and ordered that the Justice Department focus on him, along with other figures such as Teamster President Hoffa and Chicago Mafia leader Sam Giancana.

'In Marcello's case, the intent of the Kennedy administration was made known even before Inauguration Day, 20 January 1961. On 28 December 1960, the *New Orleans States-Item* reported that Attorney General-designate Kennedy was planning specific actions against Marcello. An FBI report from that period noted: "On 12 January 1961, a [source] advised that Carlos Marcello is extremely apprehensive and upset and has [been] since the *New Orleans States-Item* newspaper on 28 December 1960 published a news story reporting that . . . Robert F. Kennedy stated he would expedite the deportation proceedings pending against Marcello after Kennedy takes office in January 1961."

'The Bureau's La Cosa Nostra file for 1961 noted that Marcello flew to Washington, DC shortly after the inauguration of President Kennedy and was in touch with a number of political and business associates. While there he placed a telephone call to the office of at least one Congressman.

'Bureau records further indicate that Marcello initiated various efforts to forestall or prevent the anticipated prompt deportation action. An FBI report noted that Marcello may have tried a circuitous approach. Through a source, the Bureau learned of another Mafia leader's account of how Marcello had reportedly proceeded. Philadelphia underworld leader Angelo Bruno discussed a specific attempt by Marcello to forestall an action by the immigration authorities. According to the Philadelphia underworld leader Marcello had enlisted his close Mafia associate, Santos Trafficante of Florida, in the reported plan. Trafficante in turn contacted Frank Sinatra to have the singer use his friendship with the Kennedy family on Marcello's behalf. This effort met with failure and may even have resulted in intensified Federal efforts against Marcello. [. . .]

'On 3 March 1961, General Joseph Swing of the Immigration and Naturalization Service advised the FBI that: "The Attorney General had been emphasizing the importance of taking prompt action to deport notorious hoodlums. In this connection, the Marcello case is of particular interest. A final order of deportation has been entered against Marcello but this fact is being held in strictest confidence."

'On the afternoon of 4 April 1961, 8 years after he was ordered deported, Carlos Marcello was finally ejected from the United States.

'As he walked into the INS office in New Orleans for his regular appointment to report as an alien, he was arrested and handcuffed by INS officials. He was then [unceremoniously] rushed to the New Orleans airport and flown to Guatemala. Marcello's attorneys denounced the deportation later that day, terming it "cruel and uncivilized", and noted that their client had not been allowed to telephone his attorney or see his wife. [. . .]

'On 10 April 1961, 6 days after he was deported, the Internal Revenue Service filed a $835,396 tax lien against Marcello and his wife. On 23 April, news reports disclosed that Marcello was being held in custody by Guatemalan authorities in connection with what were reported to be false citizenship papers he had presented on arrival there 6 April. On 4 May, Guatemalan President Miguel Fuentes ordered that Marcello be expelled; he was driven to and released at the El Salvador border late that night.

'On 19 May 1961, a Federal court in Washington ruled that Marcello's deportation was fully valid and denied a motion by his attorneys that it be declared illegal. With that ruling, Marcello's re-entry to the country was prohibited.

'Less than 2 weeks later, Marcello secretly gained entry into the United States. On 2 June 1961, confirming widespread rumors that their client had somehow slipped back in, Marcello's attorneys announced he had returned and was in hiding. Federal investigators have never been able to establish in detail his means of entry.

'On 5 June 1961, after Attorney General Kennedy dispatched 20 Federal agents to Shreveport, Louisiana, to conduct a search for Marcello, the Louisiana crime leader voluntarily surrendered in New Orleans and was ordered held in an alien detention center at McAllen, Texas. On 8 June, a Federal grand jury indicted him for illegal re-entry; on 11 July, the INS ruled he was an undesirable alien and once again ordered him deported.

'On 16 June 1961, the FBI received a report that a US Senator from Louisiana might have sought to intervene on Marcello's behalf. This Senator had reportedly received "financial aid from Marcello" in the past and was sponsoring a Louisiana official for a key INS position from which assistance might be rendered. [. . .]

'On 30 October 1961, Attorney General Kennedy announced the indictment of Marcello by a Federal grand jury in New Orleans on charges of conspiracy in falsifying a Guatemalan birth certificate and committing perjury. [. . .]

'On 20 December 1961, with Marcello free on a $10,000 bond, the five-member Board of Immigration

Appeals upheld the deportation order against Marcello, denying another appeal by Marcello attorneys that it be declared invalid.

'In October 1962, a Bureau of Narcotics report described Marcello as "one of the Nation's leading racketeers" and noted that he was "currently under intense investigation by the Internal Revenue Service Intelligence Division for tax fraud". The report also noted that Marcello was then instituting a further legal step to forestall deportation. Marcello's attorneys had filed a legal writ in an effort to set aside his Federal conviction on narcotics charges from 24 years earlier. This conviction was one of the key factors in the ongoing deportation proceedings against him.

'On 31 October 1962, a Federal court ruled against Marcello's attempt to have the 1938 drug conviction nullified. The court said that his claim that he had not counsel present when he pled guilty to the narcotics charge on 29 October 1938, was false, as was his claim that he had not known of his rights and could not afford an attorney.

'On 15 February 1963, in apparent response to Attorney General Kennedy's request for continuing action against Marcello, FBI Director J. Edgar Hoover directed the New Orleans FBI office to intensify its coverage of Marcello and his organization. He ordered that a "special effort" be made to upgrade the level of the investigation of Marcello, and suggested increased use of informants as well as the possible initiation of electronic surveillance . . . Two unsuccessful attempts were made to effect such surveillance, failures attributable in all likelihood to the security system employed by Marcello at the various locations from which he operated. [. . .]

'On 4 November 1963, Marcello went on trial in New Orleans on Federal charges of conspiracy in connection with his alleged falsification of a Guatemalan birth certificate. Eighteen days later, on 22 November 1963, he was acquitted. The news of President Kennedy's murder in Dallas reached the courtroom shortly before the verdict was announced.'

The above review makes clear that by 1963, top Mafia leaders and their labor cronies had been the subjects of an unprecedented, unremitting, relentless campaign against them; a campaign which could not be terminated by merely getting rid of Robert Kennedy, who could be replaced with a like-minded person by President Kennedy, whose program this was.

The Kefauver Committee had stated among its conclusions: 'The domination of the Mafia is based fundamentally on "muscle" and "murder". The Mafia is a secret conspiracy against law and order which will ruthlessly eliminate anyone who stands in the way of its success in any criminal enterprise in which it is interested. It will destroy anyone who betrays its secrets. It will use any means available – political influence, bribery, intimidation, et cetera, to defeat any attempt on the part of law enforcement to touch its top figures.'

Information of perhaps more than passing interest to our story was provided in the testimony of Aaron Kohn to the House Select Committee. According to Kohn, the 1930 crime which resulted in his first conviction – a grocery store robbery – had been personally planned by the then 20-year-old Carlos Marcello, using an interesting method of operation: 'Marcello had shielded his own complicity in the crime by inducing two juveniles to carry out the robbery . . . Marcello and a confederate had supplied the juveniles with a gun and instructions on their "getaway". The plan had gone awry when the two were later apprehended and pressured by authorities to identify the "higher-ups".' Kohn also noted that Marcello 'was referred to as a Fagin' in press accounts at the time, in an apparent reference to the Dickens character who recruited juveniles to carry out his crimes.

Organized crime had become somewhat more sophisticated by mid-century, as the House Committee noted in its final report:

'In its investigation, the Committee noted three cases, for the purposes of illustration, in which the methodology employed by syndicate figures was designed to insulate and disguise the involvement of organized crime. These did not fit the typical pattern of mob killing, as the assassination of a President would not. While the atypical cases did not involve political leaders, two of the three were attacks on figures in the public eye.

'In the first case, the acid blinding of investigative reporter Victor Riesel in April 1956, organized crime figures in New York used a complex series of go-betweens to hire a petty thief and burglar to commit the act. Thus, the assailant did not know who had actually authorized the crime for which he had been recruited. The use of such an individual was regarded as unprecedented, as he had not been associated with the syndicate, was a known drug user, and outwardly appeared to be unreliable. Weeks later, Riesel's assailant was slain by individuals who had recruited him in the plot. [. . .]

'The second case, the fatal shooting of a well-known businessman, Sol Landie, in Kansas City, Missouri, on 22 November 1970, involved the recruitment, through several intermediaries, of four young Black men by members of the local La Cosa Nostra family. Landie had served as a witness in a Federal investigation of gambling activities directed by Kansas City organized crime leader Nicholas Civella. The men recruited for the murder did not know who had ultimately ordered the killing, were not part of the Kansas City syndicate, and had received instructions through intermediaries to make it appear that robbery was the motive for the murder. All of the assailants and two of the intermediaries were ultimately convicted.

'The third case, the shooting of New York underworld leader Joseph Columbo before a crowd of 65,000 people in June 1971, was carried out by a young Black man with a petty criminal record, a nondescript loner who appeared to be alien to the organized crime group that had recruited him through various go-betweens. The gunman was shot to death immediately after the shooting of Columbo, a murder still designated as unsolved. [. . .]

'The Committee found that these three cases, each of which is an exception to the general rule of organized crime executions, had identifiable similarities. Each case was solved, in that the identity of the perpetrator of the immediate act became known. In two of the cases, the assailant was himself murdered soon after the crime. In each case, the person who wanted the crime accomplished recruited the person or persons who made the attack through more than one intermediary. In each case, the person suspected of inspiring the violence was a member of, or connected to, La Cosa Nostra. In each case, the person or persons hired were not professional killers, and they were not part of organized criminal groups. In each case, the persons recruited to carry out the acts could be characterized as dupes or tools who were being used in a conspiracy they were not fully aware of. In each case, the intent was to insulate the organized crime connection, with a particular requirement for disguising the true identity of the conspirators, and to place the blame on generally nondescript individuals.'

BOOK 3

CHAPTER

22

Jack Ruby, Mobster

Way back in late 1946, a well-known episode in organized crime history took place. In one of the more brazen efforts made during that post-war period of criminal expansion, representatives of the Chicago Mafia who were attempting to move into Dallas, Texas, sought to facilitate the maneuver by bribing Sheriff-elect Steve Guthrie. The proposed bribe was no less than a partnership in a gambling operation to be set up and financed by the mob, and kept free of trouble and competition by the Guthrie. The episode became known because Guthrie reported it and the contact man, Paul Roland Jones, was prosecuted and convicted of attempted bribery.

The scheme was to open a nightclub or restaurant downstairs, which would serve as a front for the gambling operation upstairs. As Sheriff Guthrie recalled the event years later, the person he was constantly told would manage the 'front' was Jack Ruby.

Whether or not Ruby (born Jacob Rubinstein in Chicago, 1911) was actually involved in this scheme is no longer capable of definitive proof. It is clear, however, that Ruby and members of his family were acquainted with individuals who were involved, including Chicago gangsters who had moved to Dallas in 1946–7.

In 1947 Jack Ruby moved to Dallas and established himself as a nightclub operator. After the Silver Spur, a country and western club, he opened the Sovereign, which eventually became the Carousel Club, a striptease joint.

During his years in Chicago, Ruby had also been acquainted with David Yaras and Lenny Patrick. The House Select Committee, it said, 'established that Yaras and Patrick were, in fact, notorious gunmen, having been identified by law enforcement authorities as executioners for the Chicago mob and closely associated with Sam Giancana, the organized crime leader in Chicago . . . Yaras and Patrick are believed to have been responsible for numerous syndicate executions, including the murder of James Ragan, a gambling wire service owner. The evidence implicating Yaras and Patrick in syndicate activities is unusually reliable. Yaras, for example, was overheard in a 1962 electronic surveillance discussing various underworld murder contracts he had carried out and one he had only recently been assigned.' Ruby's relationship with Patrick himself can be traced to at least the summer of 1963, and with a Patrick associate to at least the fall of 1963. Yaras, who relocated to Miami in the late 50s, had been more of a friend to Ruby, and his brother Sam, who lived in Dallas, was acquainted with Ruby.

Among Ruby's closest friends in Dallas was Lewis McWillie, who Ruby 'idolized'. McWillie had been engaged in gambling activities all his adult life, which brought him into relationships with various organized crime and gambling figures, including R. D. Matthews, a Dallas and Las Vegas gambler; Joseph Civillo, the Dallas organized crime figure; and Sam Yaras, the brother of Dave Yaras.

In September 1958, McWillie moved to Cuba and

managed the Tropicana Casino until May 1960. He worked as a pitboss at the Capri Hotel-Casino in Cuba from May 1960 to 2 January 1961, when he left Cuba for Nevada where he worked at the Cal-Neva Lodge, and then at various Las Vegas clubs.

Shortly after Fidel Castro took over in Cuba at the beginning of 1959, Elaine Mynier, a girl-friend of Lewis McWillie and an acquaintance of Jack Ruby, took a vacation in Cuba. She carried with her a coded message from Ruby to McWillie, containing various sets of numerals and letters.

At some point thereafter, Ruby purchased in Dallas and sent to McWillie in Cuba, one or more Colt Cobra guns which McWillie had requested.

On at least three occasions in the late summer and early fall of 1959, Ruby made quick trips from Miami into Cuba, apparently as some type of courier; on one of these round trips he traveled on to New Orleans upon his return.

It appears that Ruby did not spend all his time in Cuba visiting with McWillie. On at least one occasion during his time in Cuba, he went to Trescornia, a minimum security detention camp where the Castro Government was holding those who controlled extensive gambling interests in Cuba under a policy that would subsequently lead to confiscation of all underworld holdings in Cuba.

Jack Ruby's purpose in going to Trescornia was to visit with Santos Trafficante, the Florida crime boss who had controlled mob gambling in Cuba, and who would soon be a prime figure in the upcoming CIA-Mafia plots to assassinate Castro.

BOOK 4

THE WEB TIGHTENS

BOOK 4

CHAPTER

23

Curious Activities

For someone who, out of disillusionment with Soviet life, had picked up his family and left Russia, Lee Harvey Oswald continued to manifest most remarkable interests.

He wrote to the Soviet Embassy in Washington asking how to subscribe to Russian periodicals and for information on 'any periodicals or bulletins which you may put out for the benefit of your citizens living, for a time, in the USA.' He subsequently subscribed to several Russian journals. In December 1962, the Soviet Embassy received a card in Russian, signed 'Marina and Lee Oswald,' which conveyed New Year's greetings and wishes for 'health, success and all the best' to the employees at the Embassy (an interesting personal touch, considering that there is no evidence that either Lee or Marina had ever been to or had any contact with anyone at that Embassy, other than Lee's letter asking about literature).

Soon after his return to the US in June 1962, Lee had begun again manifesting an interest in Communism. In August he subscribed to the *Worker*. He also started to correspond with the Communist Party, USA, and the

Socialist Workers Party, and he also wrote for additional literature from these organizations. In October of 1962, he attempted to join the Socialist Workers Party, but his application was not accepted since there was no chapter in the Dallas area. Undaunted, he also wrote to them offering his assistance in preparing posters; and he entered a subscription to their affiliated publication, the *Militant*. In November 1962 he also wrote to the Socialist Labor Party in New York requesting literature. He wrote also to the Communist Party and asked whether, in view of his prior defection, he should 'continue to fight, handicapped as it were by past record compete with anti-progressive forces, aboveground or should always remain in the background, i.e., underground.' The Party replied that 'often it is advisable for some people to remain in the background not underground.'

At about 9 p.m. on 10 April 1963, Major General Edwin A. Walker, the controversial hero of the right wing, was sitting at his desk on the first floor of his home in Dallas when a bullet fired from outside his home entered the room and missed him. The official reconstruction was that the gunman had rested his rifle on the fence of Walker's yard. The evidence strongly points to the probability that Oswald fired the shot.

There were no eyewitnesses to the actual shooting, but the police spoke to a teenage boy in a neighboring house who said that after hearing the shot, he saw some men speeding down the alley at the rear of Walker's home in a light green or light blue Ford, either a 1959 or 1960 model. He said he also saw another car, a 1958 Chevrolet, black with white down the side, in a church parking lot adjacent to Walker's home; the car door was open and a man was bending over the back seat as though he was placing something on the floor of the car.

On the night of the incident, police interviewed Robert Surrey, an aide to Walker. Surrey said that on

Saturday 6 April, at about 9 p.m., he had seen two men sitting in a dark purple or brown 1963 Ford at the rear of Walker's house. Surrey also said the two men got out of the car and walked around the house. Surrey said he was suspicious and followed the car, noting that it had no licence plate.

If we are to assume that this was a true assassination attempt by Oswald, we must be willing to believe that this same man who at least twice hit a moving target from a rakishly high angle across Dealey Plaza, couldn't hit a stationary target only across the yard from him. If it wasn't a true assassination attempt, then it had to be a phony designed to give some credentials to Walker or Oswald or both. Whether it was real or phony may never be known, but that is relatively unimportant.

There is a much more meaningful angle to this Walker incident – an angle which must be pondered and remembered: every bit of the credible evidence makes it absolutely clear that Lee Harvey Oswald was not acting alone!

The evidence demonstrates that there were at least three others involved with Oswald in this Walker conspiracy: there were 'some' in the car in the alley, and at least two in the car in the church parking lot where a man was putting something on the back floor (it is uncontroverted that Oswald did not drive).

During the period Oswald was in New Orleans, from the end of April to late September 1963, he was engaged in activity purportedly on behalf of the now defunct Fair Play for Cuba Committee (FPCC), an organization centered in New York which was highly critical of US policy toward the Cuban Government under Fidel Castro. In May 1963, after having obtained literature from the FPCC, Oswald applied for and was granted membership in the organization.

When applying for membership, Oswald wrote to

national headquarters that he had 'been thinking about renting a small office at my own expense for the purpose of forming a FPCC branch here in New Orleans. Could you give me a charter?' (This offer to rent an office at his own expense was being made by a man who at the most – accepting the generous financial reconstruction of the Warren Committee – ended up the month of May with a grand total of $129.58 to his name.)

The FPCC responded to the effect that even if Oswald were able to organize the few members FPCC had in the New Orleans area, he would still need an equal number of new members just to be able to conduct a legal executive board for the chapter. They also strongly recommended against opening an office for a number of reasons, not the least of which was that having an identifiable location made it too easy for the 'lunatic fringe' on the other side to make trouble. Their suggestion was to use a Post Office box instead of an address.

On 3 June 1962, Oswald opened box No. 30061 at the Lafayette Square Substation in New Orleans. However, it seems clear that this was not in response to the suggestion of FPCC. For one thing, he had already been using a PO box, having maintained one at the General Post Office while in Dallas. Moreover, on this box he now opened in New Orleans, he did not list FPCC as one of the additional names entitled to receive mail at that box; he listed only Marina Oswald and A. J. Hidell (one of Oswald's aliases).

Oswald thereafter informed national headquarters that against their advice he had decided 'to take an office from the very beginning', and that he was going to have membership cards printed, which he did. He wrote three further letters to the New York office, in one of which he discussed his activity in passing out circulars on the street.

On at least three occasions, Oswald did, in fact, distribute commercially printed literature consisting of handbills demanding 'Hands off Cuba' in large letters and application forms for his FPCC chapter. Once while doing so, he was arrested and fined for being involved in a disturbance with anti-Castro Cuban refugees. His activities received some attention in the New Orleans press, and he twice appeared on a local radio program representing himself as a spokesman for the Fair Play for Cuba Committee.

Despite these activities, the FPCC chapter which Oswald purportedly formed in New Orleans was entirely fictitious.

Nor is there any evidence that Oswald ever opened an office as he claimed to have done. Although literature he was passing out contained the rubber stamp imprint 'FPCC, 544 Camp St., New Orleans, La.', investigation has established that neither the Fair Play for Cuba Committee nor Lee Harvey Oswald ever maintained an office at that address.

This address puzzle is particularly mystifying, since Oswald was passing out literature presumably designed to win over converts to his pro-Castro group; should he win people over, presumably he would like them to contact him. Why, then, would he list on the literature an address with which he had no connection – an address where he could not be contacted – when he had a post office box he could have listed where they could have contacted him (just as headquarters had suggested). The way he did it, how would someone reading the literature bearing the 544 Camp Street address have contacted Oswald in order to join him?

The disturbance with anti-Castro Cubans referred to above was described by the Warren Commission as follows.

'On 5 August, he visited a store managed by Carlos Bringuier, a Cuban refugee and avid opponent of Castro and the New Orleans delegate of the Cuban student directorate. Oswald indicated an interest in joining the struggle against Castro. He told Bringuier that he had been a Marine and was trained in guerilla warfare, and that he was willing not only to train Cubans to fight Castro but also to join the fight himself. The next day Oswald returned to the store and left his "Guidebook for Marines" for Bringuier.

'On August 9, Bringuier saw Oswald passing out Fair Play for Cuba leaflets. Bringuier and his companions became angry and a dispute resulted. Oswald and the three Cuban exiles were arrested for disturbing the peace. Oswald spent the night in jail and was interviewed by a lieutenant of the New Orleans Police Department . . . On 16 August, Oswald, assisted by at least one other person who was a hired helper, again passed out Fair Play for Cuba literature, this time in front of the International Trade Mart. That night, television newscasts ran pictures of Oswald's activities . . . William Stuckey, a radio broadcaster with a program called *Latin Listening Post*, had long been looking for a member of the Fair Play for Cuba Commmittee to appear on his program. He learned of Oswald from Bringuier . . . Stuckey arranged for a debate between Oswald and Bringuier on a 25-minute daily public affairs program called *Conversation Carte Blanche* which took place on 21 August.'

BOOK 4

CHAPTER

24

The FBI and Oswald

The Warren Commission reasoned that Oswald had met Bringuier 'by presenting himself as hostile to Premier Castro in an apparent attempt to gain information about anti-Castro organizations operating in New Orleans'.

Perhaps so. However, infiltration is not a one-way street.

Consider, for example, the FBI's counter-intelligence program against the Communist Party (COINTELPRO). Begun in 1956, COINTELPRO was expanded by a March 1960 directive to make a greater effort to prevent Communist infiltration (COMINT). This program against the Communist Party, USA (CPUSA COINTELPRO) was supplemented by SWP COINTELPRO, initiated on 12 October 1961 and directed against the Socialist Workers Party, which was targeted because of its '"open" espousal of its lines "through running candidates for public office" and its direction and/or support of "such causes as Castro's Cuba and integration problems arising in the South".' White Hate groups including the Ku Klux Klan also merited their own COINTELPROs.

Among the favorite COINTELPRO methods was the use of fictitious organizations. The Senate Select Committee described this routine as follows.

'There are basically three kinds of "notional" or fictitious organizations. All three were used in COINTELPRO attempts to factionalize.

'The first kind of "notional" was the organization whose members were all Bureau informants. Because of the Committee's agreement with the Bureau not to reveal the identity of informants, the only example which can be discussed publicly is a proposal which, although approved, was never implemented. That proposal involved setting up a chapter of the WEB DuBois Club in a Southern city which would be composed entirely of Bureau informants and fictitious persons. The initial purpose of the chapter was to cause the CPUSA expense by sending organizers into the area, cause the Party to fund Bureau coverage of out-of-town CP meetings by paying the informants' expenses, and receiving literature and instructions. Later, the chapter was to begin to engage in deviation from the Party line so that it would be expelled from the main organization "and then they could claim to be the victim of a Stalinist-type purge". It was anticipated that the entire operation would take no more than 18 months.

'The second type of "notional" was the fictitious organization with some unsuspecting (non-informant) members. For example, Bureau informants set up a Klan organization intended to attract membership away from the United Klans of America. The Bureau paid the informant's personal expenses in setting up the new organization, which had, at its height, 250 members.

'The third type of "notional" was the wholly fictitious organization, with no actual members, which was used as a pseudonym for mailing letters or pamphlets. For instance, the Bureau sent out newsletters from something called "The Committee for Expansion of Socialist Thought in America" which attacked the CPUSA from the "Marxist right" for at least two years.'

To the discussion of this last type of 'notional', we can add that obviously the setting up of such a fictitious organization can manufacture some very nice credentials for someone looking to pass himself off as something he is not.

Passing out pro-Castro literature on the street, getting into an altercation with anti-Castro Cubans, getting arrested for same, and supporting Castro in a debate on radio will all do wonders for showcasing someone as pro-Castro.

An FBI intelligence program aimed at Castro sympathizers had originally begun in 1960. After the Bay of Pigs invasion in 1961, the FBI intensified its coverage of pro-Castro Cuban activities. Particular attention came to be paid to the Fair Play for Cuba Committee.

'FBI field offices were advised [on 27 April 1961] that "increasing anti-United States attitudes and demonstrations stemming from the Cuban situation and 'cold war' tensions are cause for concern" and that pro-Castro groups might "react militantly to an emergency situation". In particular, the activities of the Fair Play for Cuba Committee revealed "the capacity of a nationality group organization to mobilize its efforts in such a situation so as to arrange demonstrations and influence public opinion". Hence, all field offices were to "be most alert to the possibility of demonstrations by nationality groups which could lead to incidents involving violence".'

On 25 July 1961, Director Hoover submitted a report to President Kennedy's Special Assistant for National Security, McGeorge Bundy, on the status of the internal security programs of the Interdepartmental Intelligence Conference. The report (in part) stated, 'The Fair Play for Cuba Committee is the principal outlet for pro-Castro propaganda and agitation on the part of US nationals sympathetic to the Castro regime. There are indications that this organization is receiving funds from the Cuban Government. In addition, investigation has shown that this group has been heavily infiltrated by the Communist Party, USA (CPUSA), and the Socialist Workers Party (SWP) . . . In fact, some chapters of the group have been directly organized by and under the complete control of the CPUSA or the SWP.'

The FBI has consistently denied that Oswald was an undercover agent, which may well be the case. However, there are certain things which seem to have to be disregarded before wholeheartedly accepting such assurances.

Oswald's actions in 1959 (defection to the Soviet Union in 1959; informing the American Embassy in Moscow that he was going to renounce his American citizenship and apply for Soviet citizenship; and his statement that he intended to reveal radar secrets to the Soviet Union) required, per FBI procedures, that a 'security case' be opened with Oswald as the subject. That was indeed done, and the security case was, as it should have been, still open when Oswald re-defected in 1962.

The Bureau indicates that it wasn't until almost three weeks after his return from Russia that they first interviewed Oswald. This was done by Special Agents John W. Fain and B. Tom Carter at the Fort Worth FBI office on 26 June 1962, at which time they say that Oswald denied he had told State Department officials at the American Embassy in Moscow that he was going to renounce his American citizenship, apply for Soviet citizenship, and reveal radar secrets to the Soviets.

Moreover, Fain told the House Select Committee, when he asked Oswald to take a polygraph test, Oswald refused to even be polygraphed on whether he had dealings with Soviet intelligence. Fain did not report Oswald's refusal to be polygraphed when he testified before the Warren Commission on 6 May 1964, 'despite', as the Senate Committee observed, 'detailed questioning by Commission members Ford and Dulles as to the discrepancies in Oswald's statements and Fain's reaction to them'.

A second interview on 16 August 1962 (this time by Fain and Special Agent Arnold J. Brown, in the back seat of Fain's automobile) yielded similar denials.

These agents all described Oswald as giving incomplete answers and demonstrating a bad attitude towards the Bureau: he was said to be cold, arrogant, uncooperative and evasive. Despite Oswald's reported attitude and demonstrable lies, the Bureau closed the Oswald security case on 26 August 1962.

The Senate Committee commented that, 'Although wide-ranging interviews were a basic investigative technique commonly used by the Bureau to develop background information on subjects of security investigations, no neighborhood or employment sources were checked in Oswald's case, nor was his wife interviewed.

'The FBI did not interview Marina Oswald prior to the assassination' despite the existence of a Bureau program 'which monitored the activities of Soviet immigrants and repatriates to detect possible foreign intelligence ties'.

Oswald's subscribing in September 1962 to the *Worker*, which the Bureau characterized as 'an east coast Communist Newspaper', came to the attention of the New York Field Office on 28 September 1962 (presumably through surveillance at that newspaper). This act, the Bureau concedes, contradicted statements attributed to Oswald in his FBI interviews that he was 'disenchanted with the Soviet Union'. Yet despite this, Oswald's security case was not re-opened. After the assassination, FBI Assistant Director Gale agreed that had standard Bureau procedures been followed, 'In light of Oswald's defection, the case should have been re-opened at the first indication of Communist sympathy or activity (i.e., September 1962).'

Then, on 26 March 1963, the Oswald security case was suddenly re-opened, the stated basis purportedly being his subscription to the *Worker* the previous September. It is curious, however, that shortly after

Oswald received this official certification that he was a security problem, he wrote a letter to the Fair Play for Cuba Committee claiming that he had passed out FPCC literature in Dallas with a placard around his neck reading 'Hands Off Cuba – Viva Fidel'.

Despite the fact that the Oswald security case was now ostensibly re-opened as of the end of March 1963, Marina Oswald was still not interviewed by the Bureau, the alleged reason for this being that there was information that Oswald had been drinking to excess and beating his wife, and that the relevant FBI manual provision required a 'cooling off' period. After the assassination, FBI Director Hoover agreed that this could only be characterized as 'an asinine excuse', and Assistant Director Gale conceded that, in fact, 'the best time to get information from her would be after she was beaten up by her husband'.

After his arrest following the Kennedy assassination, it was found that Oswald's address book contained the name, address, telephone number and automobile licence plate number of FBI agent James P. Hosty. Approximately two to three weeks earlier, Oswald had delivered a note addressed to Hosty at the FBI office in Dallas. Hosty said the note was threatening or complaining in nature, ordering him to stop bothering Oswald's wife. And well it might have, for in this period of time Oswald made a great show of writing to the Soviet Embassy to advise them that the FBI was trying to inhibit his activities on behalf of the Fair Play for Cuba Committee.

However, we will never know what was really in Oswald's note, because following the assassination – under the order, he said, of J. Gordon Shanklin, head of the Dallas FBI office – Agent Hosty destroyed it.

BOOK 4

CHAPTER

25

Oswald and the FBI

Clearly, the FBI accounts of the various contacts make it very clear that Oswald was un-cooperative and, indeed, antagonistic toward the Bureau. He wanted nothing to do with them.

Consider, however, the testimony of a man named Adrian Alba, who told the House Select Committee that as an employee and part owner of the Crescent City Garage in New Orleans, he had, in the summer of 1963, become acquainted with Lee Harvey Oswald, who at that time worked next door at the Reily Coffee Co. Oswald had spent many of his working hours at the garage, where he read gun magazines and discussed guns with Alba.

Alba related that one day an FBI agent entered his garage and requested to use one of the Secret Service cars garaged there. The FBI agent showed Alba his credentials, and Alba allowed him to take a Secret Service car, a dark green Studebaker. Later that day or the next day, Alba says he saw the FBI agent in the car handing a white envelope to Oswald in front of the Reily Coffee Co. There was no exchange of words, Alba says, and Oswald, in a bent position, turned away trom the car window and held the envelope close to his chest as he walked to the Reily Coffee Co. Alba says he believes he observed a similar transaction a day or so later as he was returning from lunch, but on this occasion he was farther away and failed to see what was handed to Oswald.

A factor which must be considered in evaluating the credibility of Alba is the fact that he did not relate his account of the transactions between Oswald and the FBI agent when he testified before the Warren Commission in 1964. He explained to the Committee in 1978 that he first remembered these incidents in 1970, when his memory was triggered by a television commercial showing a merchant running to and from a taxi to assist a customer. Alba's failure to relate this information to the Warren Commission unarguably may be a reason in and of itself to disbelieve him. On the other hand, it doesn't necessarily mean his story is untrue, any more than the fact that agent Fain failed to tell the Warren Commission that Oswald refused a polygraph means that is not true.

However, in evaluating the FBI's story as to Oswald's dealings with them, there is an undisputed fact which must be evaluated, because it is so seemingly inconsistent with the Bureau's position that Oswald was un-cooperative, antagonistic, and wanted nothing to do with them. Given that posture, how does one rationalize the fact – which the Bureau concedes to be true – that while he was in the New Orleans jail on 10 August 1963, in relation to the altercation with the anti-Castro Cubans, Lee Harvey Oswald – by his own request – was paid an official visit by FBI agent Quigley?

Incidentally, even if it is concluded that Oswald's reported overtures to Carlos Bringuier and the anti-Castro Cubans were contrived (phony), that would not necessarily prove that Oswald was not working for the FBI.

On 23 May 1961, shortly after the Bay of Pigs, FBI field offices were instructed that 'The failure of the recent invasion attempt by Cuban rebel forces has accentuated the problem of investigating anti-Castro and pro-Castro groups and individuals in the United States. In addition to discharging our security and criminal responsibilities we are faced with the necessity of acquiring and providing other agencies informative and valid intelligence data relative to the objectives and activities of both factions as well as data regarding key personalities . . . In order to discharge these investigative and intelligence responsibilities with maximum effectiveness it is essential that particular attention be afforded the development on a broadly expanded basis of sources and informants in a position to provide knowledgeable data regarding pro-Castro and anti-Castro activities.'

The Senate Committee said: 'After the missile crisis, CIA operations against Cuba apparently decreased, while operations by Cuban exile groups on their own continued. On 18 March 1963, there was a reported attack on a Soviet vessel off the northern coast of Cuba by members of two exile groups, Alpha 66, and the Second National Front of Escambray. There was another reported attack on a Soviet vessel off the northern coast of Cuba on the evening of 26–27 March 1963, by members of another anti-Castro group, Commandos L-66.

'This apparently caused considerable concern within the US Government that such activity by Cuban exile groups could produce confrontation with the Soviets. One witness stated, "the whole apparatus of government, Coast Guard, Customs, Immigration and Naturalization, FBI, CIA, were working together to try to keep these operations from going to Cuba".

'These moves to restrict exile activities had an impact on New Orleans at the time Lee Harvey Oswald was living there. As reported on page one of the *New Orleans Times-Picayune* on 1 August 1963, the FBI seized more than a ton of dynamite, 20 bomb casings, napalm material and other devices at a home in the New Orleans area on 31 July. Newspaper interest in the seizure continued with prominent articles in the *Times-Picayune* on 2 August and 4 August. [. . .]

'Additional FBI reports provided to the Warren Commission detailed other facts connected to this anti-Castro activity in New Orleans at the time of Oswald's contact with Bringuier. On 24 July, according to FBI reports, ten Cuban exiles arrived in New Orleans from Miami. These ten joined an existing group of exiles at a "training camp" north of New Orleans, which was directed by the same individuals who were involved in procuring the dynamite the FBI seized. By late July, some 28 Cuban exiles were at the training camp, allegedly awaiting transportation to Guatemala where they would work for a lumber company.

'Some of those who owned the land on which the Cuban exiles were staying became concerned about the FBI interest in the anti-Castro activities and ordered them to leave. Carlos Bringuier was called upon to assist in getting this group back to Miami.'

The Senate Committee went on to observe, 'Although this was the extent of the Warren Commission investigation of this incident, at least one FBI report, on the seizure of materials, which was not provided the Warren Commission, raises additional questions about the purpose of Oswald's contact with Bringuier . . . A report of the Miami Office of the FBI [dated 3 October 1963] revealed some of the information the FBI had on this incident:

(1) On 14 June 1963, information was received that a group of Cuban exiles had a plan to bomb the Shell refinery in Cuba.

(2) On 15 June, United States Customs Agents seized a twin Beechcraft airplane on the outskirts of Miami, Florida, along with a quantity of explosives. [. . ., . . ., . . ., "A" and . . ., along with American . . .] were involved and detained, but not arrested, by

the United States Customs Agents. It was ascertained that [. . .] supplied the money and explosives for this operation. [He] is well known as a former gambling concession operator in Havana.

(3) On 19 July 1963, [. . .] advised that there was another plan to bomb Cuba, using bomb casings and dynamite located on the outskirts of New Orleans, Louisiana.

(4) On 31 July 1963, the Federal Bureau of Investigation (FBI) at New Orleans, Louisiana, obtained a search warrant and seized 2,400 pounds of dynamite and 20 bomb casings near Lacombe, Louisiana. This material was located on the property of [. . .], brother of [. . .], [of] Miami Beach and former operator of a casino in the Nacional Hotel, Havana, Cuba.

(5) Investigation determined that this dynamite was purchased at Collinsville, Illinois, by ["B"] for "A", who was involved in the 14 June 1963 seizures at Miami. "A" transported the dynamite to New Orleans in a rented trailer. Also involved in this bomb plot were . . .

(6) [. . .] advised on 14 June 1963, "B" of Collinsville, Illinois, recently arrived in Miami, Florida, in a Ford station wagon with a load of arms for sale. American adventurers and mercenaries, [. . .] and [. . .], took "B" around to meet the different Cuban exile leaders in Miami.

'On another occasion, an intelligence agency conducted a sensitive operation which developed information on the location of arms caches and training camps in another country. That information was given to the other country, which then raided the camps and seized the materials. Raids and seizures such as these apparently were commonplace throughout the summer and fall of 1963. Those individuals apparently sponsoring this activity were angered by these raids and seizures.'

BOOK 4

CHAPTER

26

The Return of Svengali

As discussed previously, despite what Oswald had told the Fair Play for Cuba Committee headquarters about renting an office, and despite his stamp on literature he was distributing stating that FPCC was located at 544 Camp Street, investigation following the assassination revealed that neither the FPCC nor Lee Harvey Oswald had ever rented an office at that address.

Troubled by questions such as why Oswald would list an address with which he had absolutely no relationship, the House Select Committee conducted its own investigation of the possibility of a connection between Oswald and 544 Camp Street.

It turns out that the building located at 544 Camp Street, the Newman Building, occupied a corner lot where Camp Street meets Lafayette Street. Its other entrance was addressed 531 Lafayette Street. The Camp Street address was the main entrance for two tenants who have no relation to our story.

The Lafayette Street address, however, was the main entrance of Guy Banister Associates, a private investigative firm.

Guy Banister, after a 20-year career, had retired

from the FBI in 1954 to become assistant superintendent for the New Orleans Police Department. After a falling out with the mayor of New Orleans, Banister had left public service and formed his own private detective agency.

According to FBI files, Banister had become excessively involved in anti-Communist activities after his separation from the Bureau, and testified before various investigating bodies about the dangers of Communism. Early in 1961, Banister helped draw up a charter for the Friends of Democratic Cuba, an organization set up as the fund-raising arm of Sergio Arcacha Smith's branch of the Cuban Revolutionary Council.

The FBI files also indicate that Banister was running background investigations on those Cuban students at Louisiana State University who sought to join Smith's anti-Castro group, ferreting out any pro-Castro sympathizers among them.

Also extremely active in Sergio Arcacha Smith's anti-Castro group was a man we have met previously – the man who had been Lee Harvey Oswald's commander in the Civil Air Patrol – David Ferrie.

Ferrie shared Banister's anti-Communism and anti-Castro fervor. In fact, Ferrie had actually had to be asked 'to discontinue his remarks at a speaking engagement in July 1961 before the New Orleans chapter of the Military Order of World Wars. His topic was the Presidential administration and the Bay of Pigs fiasco. The organization put a stop to Ferrie's remarks when he became too critical of President Kennedy.'

Ferrie had not bothered to renew his CAP commander charter when it ran out in 1954, although he continued to wear the insignia of the CAP on his fatigues. He did renew his commander charter in 1959, when he augmented his cadet's standard CAP rifle training by instituting an association with the New Orleans Cadet Rifle Club.

'Ferrie also started a group called the "Falcon Squadron", composed of Ferrie's closest CAP associates.

A group within this group, the "Omnipotents", was allegedly starting to train cadets in what to do in the event of a major attack on the United States.

'Ferrie's job and ownership of an airplane enabled him to travel around the country with relative ease. He told officials he frequently traveled to Texas and other parts of the South, including Miami. He also visited New York on occasion. The amount of time Ferrie spent in these cities could not be determined. In August 1959, while in Miami, Ferrie was put under a 24-hour surveillance by customs agents who believed he was involved in gun smuggling. Following a brief investigation, including a tapping of his telephone conversations, it was determined that Ferrie was not involved in any illegal activity, but merely planning an outing for his "scouts". The investigation was dropped.

'Ferrie also became involved in other activities. In 1959, he had found an outlet for his political fanaticism in the anti-Castro movement. By early 1961, Ferrie and a young man whom Ferrie had first met in the CAP, Layton Martens, were working with Sergio Arcacha Smith, head of the Cuban Revolutionary Front delegation in New Orleans.

'Ferrie soon became Smith's eager partner in counter-revolutionary activities. He reportedly built two miniature submarines, which he planned to use for an attack on Havana Harbor, obtained several rifles and mortars for the proposed invasion, and was reportedly teaching Cubans how to fly. Further, several of Ferrie's cadets claimed to have taken trips to Cuba in Ferrie's airplane.

'Ferrie was also involved with Arcacha Smith, adventurer Gordon Novel and Layton Martens in a raid on a munitions dump in Houma, Louisiana.' Others who were said to have participated in the raid, in which various weapons, grenades and ammunition were stolen, were Andrew Blackmon, a Ferrie associate and former CAP cadet, and Guy Banister, whose involvement may have been limited to storing the stolen material.

'In September 1961, the US Border Patrol received information that Ferrie was attempting to purchase a C-47 airplane for $30,000 and reportedly had a cache of arms in the New Orleans area. The report was never verified. [. . .]

'Arcacha Smith wrote to Eastern Airlines' then-president Eddie Rickenbacker on Ferrie's behalf requesting a 60- or 90-day leave with pay for full-time work for the CRC. The request was denied. Nevertheless, Ferrie's vacation in April 1961 coincided with the Bay of Pigs invasion. Ferrie's role, if any, is not known.'

Guy Banister did investigative work both directly for Ferrie and for Ferrie's lawyer, G. Wray Gill, in connection with the charges brought against Ferrie by Eastern Airlines, his employer, and by the New Orleans police alleging crimes against nature, and extortion. In return, Ferrie provided Banister research services, such as analysis of autopsy reports.

Ferrie and Banister also worked together over some period of time with attorney Gill for the defense of another of Gill's clients who was involved in a deportation case – Carlos Marcello.

'Ferrie's involvement with Marcello may have begun as early as the spring of 1961. An unconfirmed Border Patrol report of February 1962 alleges that Ferrie was the pilot who flew Marcello back into the United States from Guatemala after he had been deported in April 1961 as part of the US Attorney General Robert Kennedy's crackdown on organized crime. This may have helped Ferrie establish an enduring relationship with the Marcello organized crime family.'

The return of Marcello to the United States coincided chronologically with Ferrie's activities with the Cuban Revolutionary Council. According to Carlos Quiroga, a Cuban who had been involved with the CRC, Ferrie often provided Arcacha Smith with funds, stating 'Ferrie lent him [Arcacha Smith] money when he needed it for his family . . . He [Ferrie] had $100 bills around all the time', even after he lost his job with the airlines.

As a result of his work with Guy Banister, David Ferrie spent a good deal of time at Banister's office at the Newman Building, and he and Banister were frequent customers at Mancuso's coffee shop on the first floor. Less than a block away were the Reily Coffee Co., where Oswald worked, and the Crescent City Garage, whose owner, Adrian Alba, testified that he had often seen Oswald in Mancuso's.

Following his much-publicized altercation and subsequent debate with the anti-Castro leader, Carlos Bringuier, near the end of August 1963, Oswald largely passed out of sight in New Orleans until mid-September.

During this period, Oswald reportedly appeared in Clinton, Louisiana, where a voting rights demonstration organized by the Congress of Racial Equality was in progress. Clinton, the county seat of East Feliciana Parish, was about 130 miles from New Orleans.

'There were six witnesses in Clinton who saw Oswald there, among them a State representative, a deputy sheriff and a registrar of voters . . . In addition to the physical descriptions they gave that matched that of Oswald, other observations of the witnesses tended to substantiate their belief that he was, in fact, the man they saw. For example, he referred to himself as "Oswald", and he produced his Marine Corps discharge papers as identification.'

The reason Oswald had to produce identification was because he was applying to be registered as a voter in East Feliciana Parish. But, as far as we know, he produced legitimate identification, so that none of the papers he produced contained an address which would qualify him to be registered as a resident of East Feliciana Parish. Apparently, the pretext he offered was that he had been seeking employment at East

Louisiana State Hospital, in nearby Jackson, Louisiana, and had been told that his job would depend on his becoming a registered voter, and so he had come to Clinton for that purpose. He was, it would appear, unsuccessful in attempting to be registered as a voter in East Feliciana Parish.

'Some of the witnesses said that Oswald was accompanied by two older men whom they identified as [David] Ferrie and [a man named Clay] Shaw.'

The House Select Committee found that 'the Clinton witnesses were credible and significant . . . If the witnesses were not only truthful but accurate as well in their accounts, they established an association of an undetermined nature between Ferrie, Shaw and Oswald less than 3 months before the assassination.'

There the matter has stood since then: 'an association of an undetermined nature' involving Oswald, David Ferrie and a third man. In other words, a mystery. But perhaps there are a few potential clues that have been overlooked.

The central question would seem to be: 'Was it only a mere coincidence that a "big-city boy" like Oswald happened to be applying to be registered as a voter out in East Feliciana Parish, just at the very time that an organized Black voting registration drive was taking place in that parish?'

Perhaps so. But let's look at a little background.

The Senate Committee, in a special volume on the Federal Bureau of Investigation, relates that in the late 50s and early 60s, in addition to its own mandate, the FBI had 'the role of an investigative agency, acting for the Justice Department, required by law to serve the Civil Rights Division, which was in turn charged with the responsibility of enforcing Federal laws with respect to civil rights . . . [T]he Civil Rights Division was to enforce the Civil Rights Acts of 1957 and 1960 – a twin responsibility to go after (A) public officials who practiced racial discrimination in registration or voting, and (B) anyone, public official or private citizen, who interfered with registration or voting by threats, intimidation, or coercion by any means. [. . .]

'In 1960 the Department of Justice believed that there was massive wide-spread racial discrimination in voting in five Deep South States (Alabama, Georgia, Louisiana, Mississippi and South Carolina) and in some counties in Florida, North Carolina and Tennessee. [. . .]

'Shortly after the Civil Rights Act of 1960 went into effect, record demands were made for 15 counties in [five] states – McCormick, Hampton and Claredon Counties, South Carolina; Webster, Fayette and Early Counties, Georgia; Wilcox, Sumpter and Montgomery Counties, Alabama; East Feliciana, Quachita and East Carroll Parishes, Louisiana; and Boliva, Leflore, and Forrest Counties, Mississippi.'

By 1964, 'The result of four years of work was a tremendous accumulation of proof of racial discrimination of voting throughout the States of Alabama, Mississippi and Louisiana.'

An example of one aspect of the Bureau's activity in this field is the 27 June 1963 memorandum on the subject 'Racial Matters' which FBI Headquarters sent to the Special Agents in charge of all field offices; in part, the memorandum reads:

'In order that the Bureau's information will be complete and absolutely current, it is essential that all offices promptly [send] information concerning racial demonstrations . . . arrests arising out of racial problems, results of court action, and any other pertinent information. Steps shall be taken to furnish pertinent information so that it will be received prior to midnight on the day of occurrence . . . When activities continue throughout the night, the Bureau is to be telephonically advised of the current status of the activities before 7 a.m., Eastern Daylight Savings Time.

'Each office must also assume responsibility for following up scheduled racial activity and promptly advising the Bureau of subsequent developments.

Whenever the Bureau has been advised that a meeting, demonstration or other pertinent activity will take place, coverage must be continued and the Bureau promptly informed as to whether the anticipated activity actually occurred, and pertinent details of what transpired. If a planned racial activity is cancelled or postponed, the Bureau should also be promptly advised.'

Given the above background, together with the other information we now know about Lee Harvey Oswald, it would seem appropriate to at least entertain the following questions:

(1) Might Oswald's business in Clinton have been part of the coverage of this Black voting registration drive organized by the Congress of Racial Equality, such as is mandated in the 'Racial Matters' memo sent from FBI headquarters to all field offices only two months earlier?

(2) Might the purpose of having Oswald apply to be registered as a voter in East Feliciana Parish, be to test whether an outside white would be treated better than local Blacks?

The so-called 'Clinton Sightings' of Oswald have significance beyond the possibility that they tie the FBI to Oswald, for they rather firmly tie the supposed pro-Castro Communist, Oswald, together with the staunch anti-Communist, anti-Castro partisan, David Ferrie.

Nor is this the only evidence tying Oswald and Ferrie together in this fateful period of time. There is a fascinating link which has been largely overlooked despite the fact that there are credible witnesses to its existence.

A Ferrie associate named Layton Martens told the police that after the assassination, W. Wray Gill (Carlos Marcello's lawyer, for whom Ferrie had been doing some work) had 'come by to relay a message to Ferrie that his library card was found among Oswald's effects'. The House Select Committee dismissed this with the comment that 'Marten's story was unsubstantiated'.

However, they subsequently relate that 'Oswald's former landlady in New Orleans, Mrs Jesse Garner, told the Committee she recalled that Ferrie visited her home on the night of the assassination and asked about Oswald's library card'. And, 'A neighbor of Oswald's, Mrs Doris Eames, told New Orleans district attorney investigators in 1968 that Ferrie had come by her house after the assassination, inquiring if Mr Eames had any information regarding Oswald's library card. Eames told Ferrie he had seen Oswald in the public library but apparently had no information about the library card Oswald used.'

Ferrie's interest in this card clearly points to an active association between Oswald and Ferrie in this period of time.

BOOK 4

CHAPTER

27

Closet Anti-Communist?

The Clinton sightings are not Oswald's only possible contact with virulent anti-Castro Cuban zealots.

Antonio Veciana Blanch was the founder of Alpha 66 which, 'throughout 1962 and most of 1963, was one of the most militant of the exile groups. Its repeated hit-and-run attacks had drawn public criticism from President Kennedy in the spring of 1963, to which Veciana replied, "We are going to attack again and again"'

Veciana told the House Select Committee that originally he had been recruited to work against the Castro Government in the middle of 1960, by a man who called himself Maurice Bishop, who purported to be with a construction firm headquartered in Belgium. Veciana related that prior to the time the American Embassy in Cuba was closed in January 1961, Bishop had suggested that he go there and contact certain officials for help in his anti-Castro activity. Veciana recalled that one of the names Bishop had given him was Sam Kail.

The Committee ascertained that Colonel Sam Kail 'served as the US Army attaché at the US Embassy in

Havana from 3 June 1958 until the day the Embassy closed, 4 January 1961. His primary mission as military attaché was that of intelligence. Later, in February 1962, he was transferred to Miami where he was in charge of the unit that debriefed newly-arrived Cuban refugees. Although he reported directly to the Chief of Army Intelligence in Washington, Kail said he assumed his unit was actually functioning for the CIA.' (The Committee doesn't mention that Kail, as we know, was also involved with Clemard Charles, the friend of George de Mohrenschildt.)

Veciana says that in mid-1961 he fled Cuba because Bishop told him Castro's agents were becoming suspicious of his activities.

'Shortly after he settled in Miami, Veciana testifies, Bishop contacted him again. [. . .]

'Early in their relationship in Miami, Bishop asked Veciana to monitor the activities of an anti-Castro operation called "Cellula Fantasma". Veciana said he attended a few meetings of the group and described the operation as a leaflet-dropping mission over Cuba which involved known soldier of fortune, Frank Fiorini Sturgis [later of Watergate fame]. [. . .]'

The result of Veciana and Bishop re-establishing contact eventually led to Veciana's founding of Alpha 66 which, according to Veciana, was the brainchild of Bishop (whose main thesis was that Cuba had to be liberated by Cubans). 'Alpha 66 became one of the most active of the anti-Castro exile groups, buying guns and boats, recruiting and training commandos, and conducting numerous raids on Cuba. [. . .]'

'According to Veciana, the man behind all of Alpha 66's strategy was Maurice Bishop. Over the 12-year period of their association, Veciana estimated he met with Bishop more than 100 times . . . Besides contacts with Bishop in Havana and Miami, Veciana also had meetings with him in Dallas, Washington, Las Vegas and Puerto Rico and in Caracas, Lima, and La Paz in South America.' Veciana testified that over the years that he knew Bishop, he had 'at least five meetings with him in Dallas'.

One of these Dallas meetings, which Veciana believed 'was in late August 1963', took place 'in the lobby of a large office building in the downtown section of the city. [. . .] When Veciana arrived for the meeting, Bishop was there talking with [a young man] . . . [The young man] remained with Bishop and Veciana only for a brief time as they walked toward a nearby coffee shop . . . [The young man] then departed, and Bishop and Veciana continued their meeting alone.

'Veciana testified that he recognized the young man with Bishop as Lee Harvey Oswald after seeing photographs of him following the Kennedy assassination. There was absolutely no doubt in his mind that the man was Oswald, not just someone who resembled him. Veciana pointed out that he had been trained to remember the physical characteristics of people and that if it was not Oswald it was his "exact" double.'

In late September 1963, three men appeared at the Dallas home of Silvia Odio, a member of the Cuban Revolutionary Junta, or JURE, to ask for help in preparing a fundraising letter for JURE. The House Committee tells us Mrs Odio stated that 'two of the men appeared to be Cubans, although they also had characteristics that she associated with Mexicans. The two individuals, she remembered, indicated that their "war" names were "Leopoldo" and "Angelo". The third man, an American, was introduced to her as "Leon Oswald", and she was told that he was very much interested in the anti-Castro Cuban cause.

'Mrs Odio stated that the men told her that they had just come from New Orleans and that they were about to leave on a trip. The next day, one of the Cubans called her on the telephone and told her that it had been his idea to introduce the American into the underground "because he is great, he is kind of nuts". The Cuban also said that the American had been in the

Marine Corps and was an excellent shot, and that the American had said that Cubans "don't have any guts because President Kennedy should have been assassinated after the Bay of Pigs, and some Cubans should have done that, because he was the one that was holding the freedom of Cuba actually". Mrs Odio claimed the American was Lee Harvey Oswald.

'Mrs Odio's sister, who was in the apartment at the time of the visit by the three men and who stated that she saw them briefly in the hallway when answering the door, also believed that the American was Lee Harvey Oswald.'

The Warren Commission concluded that Mrs Odio was mistaken. They did so, not on the basis that she and her sister were not believable, but because they concluded that other evidence made it impossible for Oswald to have been in Dallas when she said this occurred. Essentially, they concluded that the event had to have happened on either the 26th or 27th of September: if on the 26th, they asserted they had firm evidence that Oswald was on a bus from Houston to Mexico City; and if on the 27th, Oswald could not have traveled from Dallas and reached Mexico City when they knew he did, unless he had private transportation. The fact is, as the House Select Committee quoted J. Wesley Liebeler, the Warren Commission assistant counsel, 'There really is no evidence at all that Oswald left Houston on that bus.'

As to having private transportation, we now know that Oswald had at least one associate, David Ferrie, who had his own airplane.

The House Select Committee stated it 'was inclined to believe Silvia Odio. From the evidence provided in the sworn testimony of the witnesses, it appeared that three men did visit her apartment in Dallas prior to the Kennedy assassination and identified themselves as members of an anti-Castro organization. Based on a judgement of the credibility of Silvia and Annie Odio, one of these men at least looked like Lee Harvey

Oswald and was introduced to Mrs Odio as Leon Oswald.'

That last sentence is really the important finding, because from at least one aspect of our inquiry, it doesn't matter if Oswald was there or not.

Once a determination is made that the Odios are truthful when they say that the man looked like and was introduced as Oswald, the implications become, if anything, more staggering if he was not there: that would mean that less than eight weeks before the assassination, these two men showcased an imposter who looked like and was passed off as Oswald – and the next day one of them called to tell Mrs Odio that this 'Oswald' was an ex-Marine who was an excellent shot and who had talked about killing Kennedy.

In mid September 1963, Lee Harvey Oswald applied for and received a Mexican tourist card. The tourist card immediately preceding his in numerical sequence was issued to William G. Gaudet, a newspaper editor. Two days later, Gaudet departed on a 3- or 4-week trip to Mexico and other Latin American countries. This happened to coincide with Oswald's visit to Mexico City between 27 September and 3 October 1963.

Gaudet, who had once been employed by the CIA, had continued thereafter to serve 'as a source of information obtained during his trips abroad' and, in addition, 'he occasionally performed errands for the Agency'. The Agency's records purport that their contacts with Gaudet ended in 1961, but he testified that they continued through at least 1969, and were never formally terminated.

'Gaudet said he could not recall whether his trip to Mexico and other Latin American countries in 1963 involved any intelligence-related activity. He was able to testify, however, that during that trip he did not encounter Oswald, whom he had previously observed on occasion at the New Orleans Trade Mart. . . Gaudet testified that he had never met Oswald, although he had known of him prior to the assassination because Oswald had distributed literature near his office. Gaudet also stated that on one occasion he observed Oswald speaking to Guy Banister on a street corner.'

While in Mexico City, Oswald visited both the Cuban and Soviet Embassies, representing that he intended to travel to the Soviet Union, and requesting an 'in-transit' Cuban visa to permit him to enter Cuba on 30 September on the way to the Soviet Union.

The evidence is, however, that what he was attempting – or wanted to appear to be attempting – was to use the in-transit visa to get into Cuba legitimately.

When Oswald left Mexico City, he went to Dallas, where he arrived on 3 October. On 9 November he sent a letter to the Soviet Embassy in Washington to 'inform [them] of recent events since my meetings with Comrade Kostin in the Embassy of the Soviet Union, Mexico City, Mexico'.

The 'recent events' amounted to a declaration that the FBI was trying to inhibit his activities: 'The Federal Bureau of Investigation is not now interested in my activities in the progressive organization "Fair Play for Cuba Committee" of which I was secretary in New Orleans (state Louisiana) since I no longer reside in that state. However, the FBI has visited us here in Dallas, Texas, on November 1st. Agent James P. Hasty [sic] warned me that if I engaged in FPCC activities in Texas the FBI will again take an "interest" in me.'

The fact is that if Oswald's Mexico trip was on the level, the FBI most certainly should have been aggressively checking up on him. 'Under the relevant FBI manual provisions then in effect, any contact such as Oswald's with the Soviet Embassy in Mexico City required that immediate investigative action at the appropriate field office be undertaken.'

Yet, 'despite the fact that both the Dallas and New Orleans field offices were aware that Oswald had been in contact with the Soviet Embassy in Mexico City, there is no evidence that either of these field offices intensified their "efforts" to locate and interview Oswald. Most surprising, however, is that the "Soviet experts" at FBI headquarters did not intensify their efforts in the Oswald case after being informed that Oswald had met with Vice Consul Kostikov at the Soviet Embassy in Mexico City. Not only were these experts familiar with Soviet activities in general, but they knew that Kostikov was a member of the KGB. Further, the Bureau's Soviet experts had reason to believe he was an agent within the KGB's Department which carries out assassination and sabotage. They were also aware that American citizen contacts with the Soviet Embassy in Mexico City were extremely rare.'

BOOK 4

CHAPTER

28

'He Is Going To Get Hit'

On September 11 1962 at Churchill Farms, his 3,000-acre swampland plantation outside New Orleans, Carlos Marcello and three associates were discussing 'the pressure law enforcement agencies were bringing to bear on the Mafia brotherhood as a result of the Kennedy administration'. One of those present was Edward Becker, a man with ties to Joseph Sica, the Mafia leader of Los Angeles, and a close friend of Carl Roppolo, reputedly Carlos Marcello's favorite nephew.

In 1969 Ed Reid, a writer on organized crime and a former editor of the *Las Vegas Sun*, published *The Grim Reapers*, which contained what Becker had told him regarding something which had occurred at that Churchill Farms meeting. Becker authenticated so much of Reid's rendition as appears below when he testified before the House Select Committee, from whose work the following excerpts are taken:

'It was then that Carlos' voice lost its softness, and his words were bitten off and spit out when mention was made of US Attorney General Robert Kennedy, who was still on the trail of Marcello:

'"Livarsi na petra di la scarpa!" Carlos shrilled the Mafia cry of revenge: "Take the stone out of my shoe!" '"Don't worry about that little Bobby son of a bitch," he shouted. "He's going to be taken care of!"

'Ever since Robert Kennedy had arranged for his deportation to Guatemala, Carlos had wanted revenge. But as the subsequent conversation . . . showed, he knew that to rid himself of Robert Kennedy he would first have to remove the President. Any killer of the Attorney General would be hunted down by his brother; the death of the President would seal the fate of his Attorney General.

'No one at the meeting had any doubt about Marcello's intentions when he abruptly arose from the table. Marcello did not joke about such things. In any case, the matter had gone beyond mere "business"; it had become an affair of honor, a Sicilian vendetta. Moreover, the conversation at Churchill Farms also made clear that Marcello had begun to plan a move. He had, for example, already thought of using a "nut" to do the job.

'Roughly 1 year later President Kennedy was shot in Dallas – 2 months after Attorney General Robert Kennedy had announced to the McClellan Committee that he was going to expand his war on organized crime. And it is perhaps significant that privately Robert Kennedy had singled out James Hoffa, Sam Giancana, and Carlos Marcello as being among his chief targets.'

Becker told the House Committee that '"Marcello was very angry" and had "clearly stated that he was going to arrange to have President Kennedy murdered in some way"; and that Marcello's statement had been made in a serious tone and sounded as if he had discussed it previously to some extent. Becker commented that Marcello had made some kind of a reference to President Kennedy's being a dog and Attorney General Robert Kennedy the dog's tail, and had said "the dog will keep biting you if you only cut off its tail", but that if the dog's head were cut off, the dog would die.

'Becker stated that Marcello also made some kind of reference to the way in which he allegedly wanted to arrange the President's murder. Marcello "clearly indicated" that his own lieutenants must not be identified as the assassins, and that there would thus be a necessity to have them use or manipulate someone else to carry out the actual crime.'

The House Committee specifically noted that 'as a consequence of his underworld involvement', Edward Becker 'had a questionable reputation for honesty and may not be a credible source of information'.

On the other hand, the House Committee commented that Jose Aleman, who testified to a similar event involving Santos Trafficante, 'appeared to be a reputable person, who did not seek to publicize his allegations, and he was well aware of the potential danger of making such allegations against a leader of La Costa Nostra'.

Trafficante, it will be remembered, had such good business ties to the anti-Castro Cuban exile community that the CIA had used him as their contact man for their Castro assassination plots. Jose Aleman was described by the Committee as 'a prominent Cuban exile'.

Aleman told the House Committee's investigators that in September 1962, Santos Trafficante met with him relative to financial difficulties Aleman was then experiencing. A relative of Aleman's had helped someone get out of a Cuban jail, and Trafficante in return was offering to arrange a loan from the Teamsters for Aleman. In the course of this meeting, Trafficante was 'talking of the many problems in the country and of Kennedy's role in causing problems generally and in particular causing problems for certain individuals'. Speaking to a Cuban exile in late 1962, Trafficante may have had good reason to believe that it was sympathetic ears which heard him assert that 'a lot of people weren't going to forget the problems Kennedy had caused them, including Hoffa. [. . .] Trafficante brought up Jimmy Hoffa's name and said Hoffa would never forgive the Kennedys for what they did to him.'

When Trafficante began to talk in specifics, Aleman at first thought Trafficante was talking about knocking Kennedy off in the next election. So Trafficante, 'trying to make Aleman realize that he was not saying Kennedy would be defeated in the 1964 election, rather that he would not make it to the election, said: ". . . You don't understand me. Kennedy's not going to make it to the election. He is going to get hit". [. . .]

'Aleman stated that during the course of the discussion, Trafficante had made clear to him that he was not guessing that the President was going to be killed. Rather he did in fact know that such a crime was being planned . . . [and] . . . Trafficante had given him the distinct impression that Hoffa was to be principally involved in the elimination of Kennedy.'

The House Committee relates that, 'On 9 November 1963 an informant for the Miami police, William Somersett, secretly recorded a conversation with a right-wing extremist named Joseph A. Milteer, who suggested there was a plot in existence to assassinate the President with a high-powered rifle from a tall building. Miami Police intelligence officers met with Secret Service agents on 12 November and provided a transcript of the Somersett recording. It read in part:
Somersett: I think Kennedy is coming here 18 November to make some kind of speech. I don't know what it is, but I imagine it will be on TV.
Milteer: You can bet your bottom dollar he is going to have a lot to say about the Cubans; there are so many of them here.
Somersett: Well, he'll have a thousand bodyguards, don't worry about that.
Milteer: The more bodyguards he has, the easier it is to get him.

Somersett: Well, how in the hell do you figure would be the best way to get him?
Milteer: From an office building with a high-powered rifle.

Somersett: They are really going to try to kill him?
Milteer: Oh, yeah; it is in the working.

Somersett: Hitting this Kennedy is going to be a hard proposition. I believe you may have figured out a way to get him, the office building and all that. I don't know how them Secret Service agents cover all them office buildings everywhere he is going. Do you know whether they do that or not?
Milteer: Well, if they have any suspicion, they do that, of course. But without suspicion, chances are they wouldn't.'

'During the meeting at which the Miami Police Department provided this transcript to the Secret Service, it also advised the Secret Service that Milteer had been involved with persons who professed a dislike for President Kennedy and were suspected of having committed violent acts, including the bombing of a Birmingham, Alabama, church in which four young girls had been killed. They also reported that Milteer was connected with several radical right-wing organizations and traveled extensively throughout the United States in support of their views. [. . .]

'[T]he information gathered "was furnished [to] the agents making the advance arrangements before the visit of the President" [to Miami on 18 November 1963]. PRS [Protective Research Section] then closed the case, and copies of its report were sent to the Chief of Secret Service and to field offices in Atlanta, Philadelphia, Indianapolis, Nashville, Washington, and Miami.

'The Milteer threat was ignored by Secret Service personnel in planning the trip to Dallas. PRS Special Agent-in-Charge Bouck, who was notified on 8

November that the President would visit Miami on 18 November, told the Committee that relevant PRS information would have been supplied to the agents conducting advance preparations for the scheduled trip to Miami, but no effort was made to relay it to Special Agent Winston G. Lawson, who was responsible for the trip to Dallas, or to Forrest Sorrels, Special Agent-in-Charge of the Dallas office. Nor were Sorrels or any Secret Service agent responsible for intelligence with respect to the Dallas trip informed of the Milteer threat before 22 November 1963.'

As part of its examination of the evidence, the House Committee discussed the following fascinating episode. On 20 November 1963, 'a woman known as Rose Cheramie, a heroin addict and prostitute with a long history of arrests, was found . . . lying on the road near Eunice, Louisiana, bruised and disoriented'. Cheramie was taken to a private hospital in Eunice, treated for minor abrasions, and the police were called.

Francis Fruge, a lieutenant with the Louisiana State Police, responded. Though the woman needed no further medical care, she appeared to be under the influence of drugs, so Fruge took her to the jail and put her in a cell to sober up. However, as the woman began to display severe symptoms of withdrawal, Fruge called a doctor, who sedated the woman, and Fruge proceeded to transport her to the State hospital in Jackson, Louisiana.

During the trip to Jackson, Fruge asked Cheramie some 'routine' questions. Fruge told the Committee, '"She related to me that she was coming from Florida to Dallas with two men who were Italians or resembled Italians. They had stopped at this lounge . . . and they'd had a few drinks and had gotten into an argument or something. The manager of the lounge threw her out and she got on the road and hitchhiked to catch a ride, and this is when she got hit by a vehicle." Fruge said the lounge was a house of prostitution called the Silver Slipper.

'Fruge asked Cheramie what she was going to do in Dallas: "She said she was going to, number one, pick up some money, pick up her baby, and to kill Kennedy."

'Fruge claimed during these intervals that Cheramie related the story she appeared to be quite lucid.' He had her admitted to the hospital late on 20 November.

While in the hospital, Cheramie reportedly told a Dr Bowers before the assassination 'that President Kennedy was going to be killed'; and after the assassination she reportedly told a Dr Weiss that 'she had worked for Jack Ruby', and that while 'she did not have any specific details of a particular assassination plot against Kennedy . . . the "word in the underworld" was that Kennedy would be assassinated. [. . .]

'On 22 November, when he heard the President had been assassinated, Fruge said he immediately called the hospital and told them not to release Cheramie until he had spoken to her. The hospital administrators assented but said Fruge would have to wait until the following Monday before Cheramie would be well enough to speak to anyone. Fruge waited.

'Under questioning, Cheramie told Fruge that the two men traveling with her from Miami were going to Dallas to kill the President. For her part, Cheramie was to obtain $8,000 from an unidentified source in Dallas and proceed to Houston with the two men to complete a drug deal. Cheramie was also supposed to pick up her little boy from friends who had been looking after him.

'Cheramie further supplied detailed accounts of the arrangement for the drug transaction in Houston. She said reservations had been made at the Rice Hotel in Houston. The trio was to meet a seaman who was bringing in 8 kilos of heroin to Galveston by boat. Cheramie had the name of the seaman and the boat he was arriving on. Once the deal was completed, the trio would proceed to Mexico.

'Fruge . . . contacted the chief customs agent in Galveston who reportedly verified the scheduled docking of the boat and the name of the seaman. Fruge believed the customs agent was also able to verify the name of the man in Dallas who was holding Cheramie's son. Fruge recalled that the customs agent had tailed the seaman as he disembarked from the boat, but then lost the man's trail. Customs closed the case. [. . .]

'During a flight from Houston, according to Fruge, Cheramie noticed a newspaper with headlines indicating investigators had not been able to establish a relationship between Jack Ruby and Lee Harvey Oswald. Cheramie laughed at the headline, Fruge said. Cheramie told him she had worked for Ruby, or "Pinky", as she knew him, at his nightclub in Dallas and claimed Ruby and Oswald "had been shacking up for years". Fruge said he called Captain Will Fritz of the Dallas Police Department with this information. Fritz answered, he wasn't interested. Fritz and the Louisiana State Police dropped the investigation into the matter.

'Four years later, however . . . during the course of the New Orleans DA's investigation . . . Fruge attempted to corroborate the version she had given him [as to how she had ended up by the side of the road, and the number and identity of her companions]. Fruge spoke with the owner of the Silver Slipper Lounge. The bar owner, a Mr Mac Manual . . . told Fruge that Cheramie had come in with two men who the owner knew as pimps engaged in the business of hauling prostitutes in from Florida. When Cheramie became intoxicated and rowdy, one of the men "slapped her around" and threw her outside.

'Fruge claims he showed the owner of the bar a "stack" of photographs and mug shots to identify. According to Fruge, the bar-owner chose the photos of a Cuban exile, Sergio Arcacha Smith, and another Cuban Fruge believed to be named Osanto.'

In 1961, Arcacha Smith had befriended David Ferrie and both were believed to have ties with Carlos Marcello. Arcacha Smith moved from the New Orleans area in 1962 to go to Miami and later to settle in

Houston. The weekend following the assassination, Ferrie took a trip to Houston and *Galveston* for a little 'rest and relaxation'.

The House Committee informs us that in Chicago, on 21 November 1963, Thomas Mosley, an FBI informant, had a conversation with 'a Cuban exile, an outspoken critic of President Kennedy named Homer S. Echevarria'. Mosley 'for some time . . . had been involved in negotiating the sale of illegal arms' with Echevarria. On 21 November, 'Echevarria had said his group now had "plenty of money" and that they were prepared to proceed with the purchases "as soon as we [or they] take care of Kennedy". [. . .]

'. . .Echevarria was a member of the 30th of November (Cuban exile) Movement . . . an associate of his who had also spoken directly with Mosley about the arms sales was Juan Francisco Blanco-Fernandez, military director for the Cuban Student Revolutionary Directorate (DRE), and that the arms purchases were being financed through Paulino Sierra Martinez, a Cuban exile who had become a Chicago lawyer. Mosley inferred from his conversation with Echevarria and Blanco that Sierra's financial backers consisted in part of "hoodlum elements" who were "not restricted to Chicago". [. . .]

'The Committee found that the 30th of November Movement was receiving financial backing through the Junta del Gobierno de Cuba en el Exilio (JGCE), a Chicago-based organization led by Sierra. JGCE was essentially a coalition of predominantly right-wing anti-Castro groups. It had been formed in April 1963 and abolished abruptly in January 1964. During its short life, JGCE apparently acquired enormous financial backing, secured at least in part from organized gambling interests in Las Vegas and Cleveland. JGCE actively used its funds to purchase large quantities of weapons and to support its member groups in conducting military raids on Cuba. The affiliates of JGCE, in addition to the 30th of November Movement, included Alpha 66, led by Antonio Veciana Blanch, and the MIRR, whose leader was the militant anti-Castro terrorist, Orlando Bosch Avila. [. . .]

'Bosch was interviewed by the Committee in Cuartel San Carlos prison in Venezuala. He is charged with complicity in the 6 October 1975 bombing of a Cuban Airlines plane which resulted in the deaths of 73 people . . . Whether or not Bosch was the principal conspirator in the bombing of the Cuban airliner, it is known that his Cuban Power movement, which merged with other Cuban activists in 1976 to form a Cuban Secret Government, engaged in acts of terrorism. This latter group was linked with numerous recent bombing incidents, an assassination attempt against Henry Kissinger, the assassination of Orlando Letelier in Washington, DC, and the bombing of the Cuban Airlines plane.'

BOOK 4

CHAPTER

29

The Assassin's Assassin

At 12.30 p.m., 22 November 1963, as the President's open limousine proceeded at approximately 11 m.p.h along Elm Street through Dealey Plaza toward the Triple Underpass, shots fired from a rifle mortally wounded President Kennedy. At 1.22 p.m. a rifle was found in the Texas School Book Depository which subsequently was identified as being owned by Lee Harvey Oswald, but by that time Oswald was already in custody. In the meantime, Oswald was involved in what has been described as his escape.

The Warren Report stated: 'The possibility that accomplices aided Oswald in connection with his escape was suggested by the testimony of Earlene Roberts, the housekeeper at the 1026 North Beckley roominghouse. She testified that at about 1 p.m. on 22 November, after Oswald had returned to the roominghouse, a Dallas police car drove slowly by the front of the 1026 North Beckley premises and stopped momentarily; she said she heard its horn several times.' Oswald hurriedly left the house, and a few seconds later, shortly after 1 p.m., she saw him standing at a bus stop in front of the house. However, the bus did not go to where the scene of action now shifted.

About a mile away, at approximately 1.15 p.m., patrolman J. D. Tippit was driving east on 10th Street. About 100 feet past Patton Avenue he stopped his vehicle and spoke to Lee Harvey Oswald, who then approached the car and engaged in some conversation with Tippit. Tippit got out and started to walk around the front of the car. As Tippit reached the left front wheel, Oswald pulled out a revolver and shot Tippit dead. About a half-hour later, Oswald was arrested while sitting in the Texas Theater.

Two days later, as Oswald was being brought through the basement of the Dallas Police Station to be transferred to the county jail, Jack Ruby shot and killed Lee Harvey Oswald. Ruby would later explain that he had killed Oswald to spare Jackie Kennedy from having to return for Oswald's trial.

Perhaps Ruby's concern for Jackie was the reason he killed Oswald. However, there is evidence which points to the more troubling possibility that Ruby's role was to shut Oswald's mouth (as we saw in the Joe Columbo assassination and the Victor Reisel blinding, discussed in Chapter 21).

If this second scenario is correct, two of the questions which immediately follow are:

For whom was Ruby acting? and, Was Ruby the only one who had been given the task of getting rid of Oswald?

The House Select Committee investigated and reported on a number of intriguing relationships of Jack Ruby.

Since 14 October, the very same day on which Ruth Payne called Roy Truly at the Texas School Book Depository, Lee Harvey Oswald had been living at Earlene Roberts' home in the Oak Cliff section of Dallas, and maintaining a Post Office box at the terminal annex. Coincidentally enough, Jack Ruby also lived in the Oak Cliff section of Dallas and had a Post Office box at the terminal annex. A fellow boarder at Oswald's roominghouse, John Carter, was friendly with a close friend and employee of Ruby, Wanda Killam. Bertha Cheek, the sister of Oswald's landlady, visited Jack Ruby at his nightclub on 18 November 1963.

Jack Ruby's closest friend, to whom he spoke every day, was Ralph Paul. Ruby was constantly indebted to Paul for loans to operate his nightclubs, and Paul actually held a half interest in the Carousel until early 1964. Ruby became friendly with a good friend of Paul's, Austin Cook, a member of the ultra-conservative John Birch Society, and the owner of Austin's Barbeque. For about three years prior to the assassination, Cook had been employing a moonlighting Dallas policeman as a security guard at Austin's Barbeque. The policeman's name was J. D. Tippett.

Tippit's tie-in to friends of Jack Ruby would seem to permit at least the speculative query: Was Tippit's contact with Oswald shortly after the assassination merely a chance encounter, or did Tippit have a mission which Oswald sensed and reacted to?

As noted earlier, there is evidence that in the summer of 1963, Jack Ruby had placed a call to Chicago to Lenny Patrick, who was said to be 'one of the Chicago Mafia's leading assassins, responsible, according to Federal and State law enforcement files, for the murders of over a dozen mob victims'. Patrick was not the only unsavory character to whom Ruby spoke.

The House Committee undertook an extensive study of Ruby's telephone activity, from which the following excerpts are taken.

'A chronological consolidation of the telephone calls made by [Jack] Ruby from the five separate business and home telephones he used uncovered a significant increase in the number of calls made in October and November 1963. The average number leapt from around 25 to 35 in the months of May through September to approximately 75 in October and approximately 96 during the first 3½ weeks of November. [. . .]

'An extensive computer analysis of his telephone toll

records for the month prior to the President's assassination revealed that he either placed calls to or received calls from a number of individuals who may be fairly characterized as having been affiliated, directly or indirectly, with organized crime. These included Irwin Weiner, a Chicago bondsman well-known as a frontman for organized crime and the Teamsters Union; Robert "Barney" Baker, a lieutenant of James R. Hoffa and associate of several convicted organized crime executioners; Nofio J. Pecora, a lieutenant of Carlos Marcello, the Mafia boss in Louisiana; Harold Tannenbaum, a New Orleans French Quarter nightclub manager who lived in a trailer park owned by Pecora; McWillie, the Havana gambler; and Murray "Dusty" Miller, a Teamster deputy of Hoffa and associate of various underworld figures. [. . .]

'Between June and August of 1963, Jack Ruby placed seven long distance calls to Lewis J. McWillie . . . In 1959, Ruby had visited Lewis McWillie in Havana, where McWillie was working in an organized crime-controlled casino. Jack Ruby's phone calls to McWillie occurred on 27 June, 2 September (two calls), 4 September, 19 September, 20 September and 22 September. The first two calls were placed to McWillie's home number, the remaining five calls were to McWillie's place of business, the Thunderbird Casino in Las Vegas. [. . .]

'On the afternoon of 26 October 1963, Jack Ruby placed a long distance phone call to Irwin S. Weiner in Chicago, with whom he spoke for 12 minutes. Weiner was and is a prominent bondsman in Chicago, who has been closely linked with such figures as James Hoffa, Santos Trafficante, Sam Giancana, Paul and Allen Dorfman. Weiner, according to Federal and State law enforcement files, is alleged to have served as a key functionary in the longtime relationship between the Chicago Mafia and various corrupt union officials, particularly during Hoffa's reign as President of the Teamsters Union. Additionally, Weiner has been involved in a business relationship with two men long identified as executioners for the Chicago Mafia – Felix "Phil" Alderisio and Albert "Obie" Frabotta. [. . .]

'At 9.13 p.m., 30 October 1963, 4 days after his call to Irwin Weiner, Jack Ruby placed a call to the Tropical Court Tourist Park, a trailer park in New Orleans. The number Ruby called, 242–5431, was listed as the business office of the Tropical Court, and the duration of the call was one minute. In a partial compilation of numbers called by long distance by Ruby, transmitted to the Warren Commission by the FBI in early 1964, a notation was made indicating that this Ruby call to the Tropical Court went to N. J. Pecora. The Warren Commission did not, however, interview or investigate Pecora and made no mention of him in its Report.

'Nofio J. Pecora, alias Joseph O. Pecoraro, was the owner of the Tropical Court Tourist Park. He ran the park from a one-man office located on the premises, the office Ruby had called on 30 October. Pecora, a former heroin smuggler, was alleged to be a close associate of Carlos Marcello. The FBI, Justice Department, and Metropolitan Crime Commission of New Orleans have identified Pecora as one of Marcello's three most trusted aides. Law enforcement surveillance reports have indicated a particularly close Marcello-Pecora relationship during the early 1960s, with Pecora always close at hand at Marcello's Town and Country Motel headquarters on the outskirts of New Orleans.

'On 7 November 1963 Ruby received a collect call from Robert G. (Barney) Baker of Chicago. The call lasted 17 minutes. Baker is said to have been a top lieutenant and reputed "enforcer" for Teamster President James Hoffa. A former boxer and ex-convict, Baker was perhaps Hoffa's best known assistant during the McClellan Committee investigation of labor racketeering in the late 1950s. The Senate investigation, coordinated by then chief counsel Robert F. Kennedy, had detailed Baker's role as Hoffa's personal liaison to various leading Mafia figures. In his McClellan testimony, Baker recited a long list of Mafia hit men with whom he had been associated. In 1960, Robert F. Kennedy wrote of Baker, "Sometimes the mere threat of his presence in a room was enough to silence the men who would otherwise have opposed Hoffa's reign." [. . .]

'On 8 November 1963, the day after he received the call from Barney Baker, Ruby placed a call to Murray W. (Dusty) Miller at the Eden Roc Hotel in Miami. The call lasted four minutes. Dusty Miller was another key lieutenant of Teamster President James Hoffa, and as head of the powerful southern conference of the union, he was regarded as a possible successor to Hoffa. Miller, who had been a Teamster leader in Dallas, was associated with numerous underworld figures. [. . .]

'At 5.22 p.m., 8 November 1963, 31 minutes after he called Dusty Miller, Jack Ruby placed a call to Barney Baker in Chicago. This call lasted 14 minutes. [. . .]

'The Committee found that the evidence surrounding the calls was generally consistent – at least as to the times of their occurrence – with the explanation that they were for the purpose of seeking assistance in a labor dispute. Ruby, as the operator of two nightclubs, the Carousel and the Vegas, had to deal with the American Guild of Variety Artists (AGVA), an entertainers' union. Ruby did in fact have a history of labor problems involving his striptease performers, and there was an ongoing dispute in the early 1960s regarding amateur performers in Dallas area nightclubs. Testimony to the Committee supported the conclusion that Ruby's phone calls were, by and large, related to his labor troubles. In light of the identity of some of the individuals, however, the possibility of other matters being discussed could not be dismissed.

'In particular, the Committee was not satisfied with the explanations of three individuals closely associated with organized crime who received telephone calls from Ruby in October or November 1963.

'Weiner, the Chicago bondsman, refused to discuss his call from Ruby on 26 October 1963 with the FBI in 1964, and he told a reporter in 1976 that the call had nothing to do with labor problems. In his executive session testimony before the Committee, however, Weiner stated that he had lied to the reporter, and he claimed that he and Ruby had, in fact, discussed a labor dispute. The Committee was not satisfied with Weiner's explanation of his relationship with Ruby. Weiner suggested Ruby was seeking a bond necessary to obtain an injunction in his labor troubles, yet the Committee could find no other creditable indication that Ruby contemplated seeking court relief, nor any other explanation for his having to go to Chicago for such a bond.

'Barney Baker told the FBI in 1964 that he had received only one telephone call from Ruby (on 7 November 1963) during which he had curtly dismissed Ruby's plea for assistance in a nightclub labor dispute. The Committee established, however, that Baker received a second lengthy call from Ruby on 8 November. The Committee found it hard to believe that Baker, who denied the conversation ever took place, could have forgotten it.

'The Committee was also dissatisfied with the explanation of a call Ruby made on 30 October 1963, to the New Orleans trailer park office of Nofio J. Pecora, the long-time Marcello lieutenant. Pecora told the Committee that only he would have answered his phone and that he never spoke with Ruby or took a message from him. The Committee considered the possibility that the call was actually for Harold Tannenbaum, a mutual friend of Ruby and Pecora who lived in the trailer park, although Pecora denied he would have relayed such a message.

'Additionally, the Committee found it difficult to dismiss certain Ruby associations with the explanation that they were solely related to his labor problems. For example, James Henry Dolan, a Dallas AGVA representative, was reportedly an acquaintance of both

Carlos Marcello and Santos Trafficante. While Dolan worked with Ruby on labor matters, they were also allegedly associated in other dealings, including a strong-arm attempt to appropriate the proceeds of a one-night performance of a stage review at the Adolphus Hotel in Dallas called *Bottoms Up*. The FBI, moreover, has identified Dolan as an associate of Nofio Pecora. The Committee noted further that reported links between AGVA and organized crime figures have been the subject of Federal and State investigations that have been underway for years. The Committee's difficulties in separating Ruby's AGVA contacts from his organized crime connections was, in large degree, based on the dual roles that many of his associates played. [. . .]

'According to FBI records, AGVA has been used frequently by members of organized crime as a front for criminal activities.

'In assessing the significance of these Ruby contacts, the Committee noted, first of all, that they should have been more thoroughly explored in 1964 when memories were clearer and related records (including, but not limited to, additional telephone toll records) were available. Further, while there may be persuasive arguments against the likelihood that the attack on Oswald would have been planned in advance on the telephone with an individual like Ruby, the pattern of contacts did show that individuals who had the motive to kill the President also had knowledge of a man who could be used to get access to Oswald in the custody of the Dallas police. In Ruby, they also had knowledge of a man who had exhibited a violent nature and who was in serious financial trouble. The calls, in short, established knowledge and possible availability, if not actual planning.'

The House Committee reported that it had 'also investigated the relationship between Ruby and the Dallas Police Department to determine whether members of the department might have helped Ruby get access to Oswald for the purpose of shooting him. Ruby had a friendly and somewhat unusual relationship with the Dallas Police Department, both collectively and with individual officers, but the Committee found little evidence of any significant influence by Ruby within the force that permitted him to engage in illicit activities. Nevertheless, Ruby's close relationship with one or more members of the police force may have been a factor in his entry to the police basement on 24 November 1963.

'Both the Warren Commission and a Dallas Police Department investigative unit concluded that Ruby entered the police basement on 24 November 1963, between 11.17 a.m., when he apparently sent a telegram, and 11.21, when he shot Oswald, via the building's Main Street ramp as a police vehicle was exiting, thereby fortuitously creating a momentary distraction. The Committee, however, found that Ruby probably did not come down the ramp, and that his most likely route was an alleyway located next to the Dallas Municipal Building and a stairway leading to the basement garage of police headquarters.

'The conclusion reached by the Warren Commission that Ruby entered the police basement via the ramp was refuted by the eyewitness testimony of every witness in the relevant area, only Ruby himself excepted. It was also difficult for the Committee to reconcile the ramp route with the 55-second interval (derived from viewings of the video tapes of the Oswald murder) from the moment the police vehicle started up the ramp and the moment Ruby shot Oswald. Ruby would have had to come down the ramp after the vehicle went up, leaving him less than 55 seconds to get down the ramp and kill Oswald. Even though the Warren Commission and the Dallas police investigative unit were aware of substantial testimony contradicting the ramp theory, they arrived at their respective conclusions by relying heavily on Ruby's own assertions and what they perceived to be the absence of a plausible alternative route.

'The Committee's conclusion that Ruby entered from the alley was supported by the fact that it was much less conspicuous than the alternatives, by the lack of security in the garage area and along the entire route, and by the testimony concerning the security of the doors along the alley and stairway route. This route would also have accommodated the 4-minute interval from Ruby's departure from a Western Union office near police headquarters at 11.17 a.m. to the moment of the shooting at 11.21.'

The House Committee declared that, 'Based on a review of the evidence, albeit circumstantial, the Committee believed that Ruby's shooting of Oswald was not a spontaneous act, in that it involved at least some premeditation. Similarly, the Committee believed that it was less likely that Ruby entered the police basement without assistance, even though the assistance may have been provided with no knowledge of Ruby's intentions. The assistance may have been in the form of information about plans for Oswald's transfer or aid in entering the building or both.

'The Committee found several circumstances significant in its evaluation of Ruby's conduct. It considered in particular the selectively recalled and self-serving statements in Ruby's narration of the events of the entire 22–24 November weekend in arriving at its conclusions. It also considered certain conditions and events.

'The Committee was troubled by the apparently unlocked doors along the stairway route and the removal of security guards from the area of the garage nearest the stairway shortly before the shooting; by a Saturday night telephone call from Ruby to his closest friend, Ralph Paul, in which Paul responded to something Ruby said by asking him if he was crazy; and by the actions and statements of several Dallas police officers, particularly those present when Ruby was initially interrogated about the shooting of Oswald.

'There is also evidence that the Dallas Police Department withheld relevant information from the Warren Commission concerning Ruby's entry to the scene of the Oswald transfer. For example, the fact that a polygraph test had been given to Sergeant Patrick Dean in 1964 was never revealed to the Commission, even though Dean was responsible for basement security and was the first person to whom Ruby explained how he had entered the basement. Dean indicated to the Committee that he had "failed" the test, but the Committee was unable to locate a copy of the actual questions, responses and results.

'The Committee noted that other Ruby activities and movements during the period immediately following the assassination – on 22 and 23 November – raised disturbing questions. For example, Ruby's first encounter with Oswald occurred over 36 hours before he shot him. Ruby was standing within a few feet of Oswald as he was being moved from one part of police headquarters to another just before midnight on 22 November. Ruby testified that he had no trouble entering the building, and the Committee found no evidence contradicting his story. The Committee was disturbed, however, by Ruby's easy access to headquarters and by his inconsistent accounts of his carrying a pistol. In an FBI interview on 25 December 1963, he said he had the pistol during the encounter with Oswald late in the evening of 22 November. But when questioned about it by the Warren Commission, Ruby replied, "I will be honest with you. I lied about it. It isn't so, I didn't have a gun."

'Finally, the Committee was troubled by reported sightings of Ruby on Saturday, 23 November, at Dallas police headquarters and at the county jail at a time when Oswald's transfer to the county facility had originally been scheduled. These sightings, along with one on Friday night, could indicate that Ruby was pursuing Oswald's movements throughout the weekend.'

'The Committee also questioned Ruby's self-professed motive for killing Oswald, his story to the Warren Commission and other authorities that he did it out of sorrow over the assassination and sympathy for the President's widow and children. Ruby consistently claimed that there had been no other motive and that no one had influenced his act. A handwritten note by Ruby, disclosed in 1967, however, exposed Ruby's explanation for the Oswald slaying as a fabricated legal ploy. Addressed to his attorney, Joseph Tonahill, it told of advice Ruby had received from his first lawyer, Tom Howard, in 1963: "Joe, you should know this. Tom Howard told me to say that I shot Oswald so Caroline and Mrs Kennedy wouldn't have to come to Dallas to testify. OK?"'

'The Committee examined a report that Ruby was at Parkland Hospital shortly after the fatally wounded President had been brought there on 22 November 1963. Seth Kantor, a newsman then employed by Scripps-Howard who had known Ruby, later testified to the Warren Commission that he had run into him at Parkland and spoken with him shortly before the President's death was announced. While the Warren Commission concluded that Kantor was mistaken, the Committee was impressed by the opinion of Burt W. Griffin, the Warren Commission counsel who directed the Ruby investigation and wrote the Ruby section of the Warren report. Griffin told the Committee he had come to believe, in light of evidence subsequently brought out, that the Commission's conclusion about Kantor's testimony was wrong.'

Subsequent to Ruby's apprehension, he was given a polygraph examination. There is general agreement by everyone who has reviewed the test (Warren Commission,

FBI, House Committee) that it was unsatisfactorily administered. However, while unable to interpret the test as an overall piece, the panel retained by the House Committee did observe – contrary to what had been concluded in 1964 – that, because it produced the largest valid GSR reaction together with a constant suppression, Ruby was possibly lying when he answered 'No' to the question 'Did you assist Oswald in the assassination?'

The Committee noted several other areas of telephone contact or relationship of probative interest. Of note is the fact that they are not likely to be explainable on the basis of Ruby's labor problems.

'The Committee found that Barney Baker had placed a telephone call to another onetime associate of Jack Ruby on the evening of 21 November 1963. The person Baker called was David Yaras of Miami. Yaras was a close friend and partner of Lenny Patrick. He had also been acquainted with Ruby during their early years in Chicago. Like Lenny Patrick, Dave Yaras has served, it is alleged, as a key lieutenant of Chicago Mafia leader Sam Giancana, reputedly as an executioner.'

The Committee also found that shortly before midnight on 21 November 1963, Jack Ruby had drinks at the Cabana Motel with Jean Aase West, and a mutual friend, Lawrence Meyers. The Committee further found that, while in Chicago on 24 September 1963, Miss West had received a 15-minute telephone call from an 'investigator' working for New Orleans Mafia boss, Carlos Marcello.

The man who placed that call to Chicago, to this person who was in Dallas with Ruby on the eve of the assassination, was the staunch anti-Communist, anti-Castro activist who had once been Oswald's CAP squadron leader, the man who only weeks before this call had been with Oswald in Clinton, Louisiana – David Ferrie.

BOOK 4

CHAPTER

30

The Rosetta Stone

The overwhelming and conclusive evidence is that President John F. Kennedy had at least two sets of bitter enemies within the US, each of which had the means, motive and opportunity to assassinate him; and each of which had an unbroken history demonstrating absolutely no reluctance to the use of force. The evidence is inescapable that these two groups – organized crime and anti-Castro Cuban exiles – owed their very existence to their continued use of violence.

That is not to say that all members of organized crime or all anti-Castro Cuban exiles were involved in the Kennedy assassination. No such finding is warranted – or necessary.

However, the proof is that important elements from each group were involved in very specific planning to murder the President.

Importantly, those very same elements had a common bond, having been united (to provide their unique services) by the CIA, some of whose agents secretly continued to encourage their projects long after being ordered to stop them.

The evidence is, to say the least, abundant that the

CIA, and indeed all of the American intelligence community including the FBI, routinely utilized what can only be described as a motley group of people to perform various services for them. Here in our own little story we find that Congressional investigations have identified the following people to have been involved with American intelligence: Yuri Nosenko, a KGB officer; Richard E. Snyder, consular officer in the US Embassy in Moscow; Dr Alexis H. Davidson, US Embassy physician in Moscow; George de Mohrenschildt, friend of Oswald; John Rosselli, Mafia; Sam Giancana. Mafia; Santos Trafficante, Mafia; Guy Banister, anti-Castro activist; Sergio Arcacha Smith, anti-Castro activist; Antonio Veciana Blanch, anti-Castro activist; Homer S. Echevarria, anti-Castro activist; and Orlando Bosch Avila, anti-Castro activist, amongst others.

Even if one rejects the implication pointed to in this book that Oswald was himself an American intelligence agent, it seems unarguable that he was not the loner he has been made out to be, and that he was associated with people who were, at the least, involved on the periphery of American intelligence.

As the Kennedy years proceeded, the Mafia and the anti-Castro activists – who might be forgiven for believing that their CIA activities had earned them the right to be ignored – instead found themselves more and more the primary targets of relentless and unmerciful campaigns instigated and prosecuted by the Kennedy administration.

Given the fact that these were people who truly existed both by and for violence, it should not be surprising that certain elements of these deadly enemies of the President might see his assassination as the answer to their problems.

Those who challenge the official findings by questioning whether Oswald pulled the trigger are probably missing the central issue, for even if he did (as the proof suggests), the more important point is that the evidence also rather strongly indicates that he was the designated 'nut', specifically chosen to be identified and then eliminated.

If we eliminate Jack Ruby's alleged reason for killing Oswald (the lawyer-inspired 'protect Jackie'), we are left in our search for his motive with the evidence of Ruby's mob background and associates – that, and our common sense.

Indeed, the question of Ruby's motive may well be the 'Rosetta Stone' of the Kennedy assassination, for if Ruby was acting for others, those others had to have a reason to want Oswald eliminated.

Those who are satisfied with a 'non-conspiratorial' explanation for Ruby's rub-out of Oswald will probably have wasted their time reading this book. Those who remain unsatisfied with such a seemingly illogical rationalization might, it is hoped, have had their interest piqued by the material discussed in this book and might, it is further hoped, contribute their own thoughts towards a general rethinking of this web.

SOURCES

Warren Report   *Report of the President's Commission on the Assassination of President John F. Kennedy*, published by the US Government Printing Office (1964).

Assassinations   *Alleged Assassination Plots Involving Foreign Leaders*, conducted by the Select Committee to Study Governmental Operations with respect to Intelligence Activities, United States Senate, published by the US Government Printing Office (1975).

Senate Select   *Investigation of the Assassination of President John F. Kennedy*, conducted by the Senate Select Committee to Study Governmental Operations with Respect to Intelligence Activities, United States Senate, published by the US Government Printing Office (1976).

House Select   *Investigation of the Assassination of President John F. Kennedy*, conducted by the Select Committee on Assassinations of the US House of Representatives, published by the US Government Printing Office (1979).

NOTES

Chapter 1

Exchange Alley's character –
House Select, Vol. IX, pp. 93–4;

Background of Marguerite and Lee –
Warren Report, Chap. VII &
Appendix XIII.

Chapter 2

Connections with organized crime
and Carlos Marcello –
House Select, Vol IX, pp. 95–103 &
115–17.

Chapter 3

Civil Air Patrol and David Ferrie –
House Select, Vol. IX, pp. 103–15, &
Vol. X, pp. 106–8.

Chapter 4

Communist Literature, Socialist
Party, possible motives –
Warren Report – Chap. VII & App.
XIII; *Senate Select* – Book III, pp.
3–19; *House Select* – Report, pp.
241, & Vol. X, pp. 106–8;

I Led Three Lives –
Marguerite Oswald's testimony
before the Warren Commission.

Chapter 5

Marine Corps and discharge –
Warren Report, App. XIII;
House Select, Report, pp. 220–1;

U-2 Spyplane –
House Select, Vol. XII, p. 479.

Chapter 6

Defection –
Warren Report, App. XIII;
House Select, Report, pp. 211–12.

Chapter 7

Russia –
Warren Report, Chap. VII, App.
XIII, App XV;

Poor shot –
House Select, Vol. XII, p. 513.

Chapter 8

Oswald's 'Historic Diary' –
House Select, Vol. VIII, pp. 223–7 &
232–8.

**Chapters
9 to 13**

Yuri Nosenko –
House Select, Vol. II, pp. 436–87, &
Vol. XII, pp. 475–570;

Polygraph –
House Select, Vol VIII, p. 187–96;

Mr D. C. –
House Select, Vol. XII, pp. 571–
644;

John Hart –
House Select, Vol. II, pp. 487–
536;

Conclusion that Nosenko lied and
speculation as to why –
House Select, Report, pp. 101–2;

Richard Helms –
House Select, Vol IV, pp. 1–250;

David Murphy –
House Select, Vol XII, p. 533.

Chapter 14

CIA –
House Select, Report, pp. 197–225.

Chapter 15

Oswald's return –
Warren Report, App. XIII;

George de Mohrenschildt –
House Select, Vol. XII, pp. 47–69.

Chapter 16

Covert Action –
Assassinations, pp. xiii, 9–10, 13–69
(Lumumba), and 191–215 (Trujillo).

Chapter 17

CIA/Mafia/Cuban Exile plots against
Castro –
Assassinations, pp. 71–180;
House Select, Vol. X, pp. 147–95.

Chapter 18

Attorney Edward Morgan –
Senate Select, Vol. V, pp. 80–6.

Chapter 19

Anti-Castro Cubans, origins, feelings toward JFK –
House Select, Vol. X, pp. 5–15;

JFK vow to 'splinter' the CIA –
House Select, Report, p. 25.

Chapter 20

Domestic enemies –
House Select, Report, pp. 24–35.

Chapter 21

Organized crime –
House Select, Vol. IX, pp. 6–60, and
Report pp. 33–4;

Hoffa plot –
House Select, Report, pp. 176–7;

Carlos Marcello –
House Select, Vol. IX, pp. 61–92.

Chapter 22

Jack Ruby's mob background –
House Select, Vol. IX, p. 802–5, and
Report, pp. 149–53.

Chapter 23   Oswald/Walker incident/ Fair Play for Cuba Committee –
Warren Report, Chap. IV and App. XIII.

Chapter 24   FBI –
Senate Select, Book III, pp. 17–19, 45–6, 427–69; Book V, pp. 87–90; Report, pp. 95–7;
House Select, Report, pp. 190, 195.

Chapter 25   FBI (continued) –
Senate Select, Vol. III, p. 467; Report, pp. 11–13;
House Select, Report, pp. 185–94.

Chapter 26   Oswald's anti-Communist, anti-Castro connections –
House Select, Vol. X, pp. 105–22 (David Ferrie), 123–36 (544 Camp Street).

Clinton sightings –
House Select, Report, pp. 142–3; *Senate Select*, Vol VI, pp. 888–991 (FBI/voting rights).

Chapter 27   Oswald's anti-Castro connections (continued) –
Senate Select, Report, p. 92; *House Select*, Vol. X, pp. 37–56 (Veciana); 19–35 (Odio); Report, pp. 137–139 (Odio); 218–19 (Gaudet).

Chapter 28   Threats –
House Select, Vol IX, pp. 75–6 (Marcello); Report, pp. 171–2 (Marcello); 173–4 (Aleman); 232–3 (Milteer); 236–7 (Echevarria); Vol. X, pp. 89–91 (Bosch); 199–203 (Rose Cheramie).

Chapter 29   *Warren Report*, Chapter VI.

Chapter 23

Oswald/Walker incident/ Fair Play for Cuba Committee –
Warren Report, Chap. IV and App. XIII.

Chapter 24

FBI –
Senate Select, Book III, pp. 17–19, 45–6, 427–69; Book V, pp. 87–90; Report, pp. 95–7; *House Select*, Report, pp. 190, 195.

Chapter 25

FBI (continued) –
Senate Select, Vol. III, p. 467; Report, pp. 11–13; *House Select*, Report, pp. 185–94.

Chapter 26

Oswald's anti-Communist, anti-Castro connections –
House Select, Vol. X, pp. 105–22 (David Ferrie), 123–36 (544 Camp Street).

Clinton sightings –
House Select, Report, pp. 142–3; *Senate Select*, Vol VI, pp. 888–991 (FBI/voting rights).

Chapter 27

Oswald's anti-Castro connections (continued) –
Senate Select, Report, p. 92; *House Select*, Vol. X, pp. 37–56 (Veciana); 19–35 (Odio); Report, pp. 137–139 (Odio); 218–19 (Gaudet).

Chapter 28

Threats –
House Select, Vol IX, pp. 75–6 (Marcello); Report, pp. 171–2 (Marcello); 173–4 (Aleman); 232–3 (Milteer); 236–7 (Echevarria); Vol. X, pp. 89–91 (Bosch); 199–203 (Rose Cheramie).

Chapter 29

Warren Report, Chapter VI.
Jack Ruby –
House Select, Report, pp. 148–9 (Ruby and Oswald); Vol. XII, pp. 41–2 (Ruby/Cook/Tippit); VIII, pp. 217–8 (polygraph); Vol. IX, pp. 188–96 (Ruby's telephone calls); 127–32 (police headquarters).